MINDFIT MINDSET

THE MINDSET OF WEIGHT LOSS

JENNA RIGBY

AND CO.

CONTENTS

DEDICATION

I dedicate this book to my five amazing little humans who inspire me every day to be better, do better and stay focused. For every hour I work, know I do it for you.

A special thank you to all those who helped me stay smiling the last nine months. You know who you are, and I will be forever grateful to have you in my life

ABOUT THE AUTHOR

Jenna Rigby is an Award–Winning Weight Loss Expert helping women globally create a body they love through exercise and Positive Psychology.

A passionate writer, Jenna has been featured in publications such as *Women's Health*, *Marie Claire*, and *Woman & Home* sharing her tips of advice on healthy living. Her collaboration with *Reebok* has seen her expertise and research shared worldwide. She regularly writes for newspapers *The Huffington Post* and *The Metro* and has also been featured in *Daily Mail*.

Often described as a 'yummy mummy', Jenna has five children and runs her own boutique fitness studio, Glamfit Studios. She inspires and supports busy mums in prioritising self-care and staying fit and healthy. Offering tailored twelve-week body transformation packages she helps women change their lifestyle, mindset and eating habits in her private studio.

A registered member of the Positive Psychology Guild, Jenna shares with her audience how to create the healthiest version of yourself and flourish both on the inside and the outside. She regularly presents mindset workshops, wellbeing courses and offers her expertise in the links to weight loss.

You can find out more about Jenna and follow her here:

www.mindfitmindset.com

facebook.com/jennarigby

twitter.com/glamfitstudios

instagram.com/glamfitstudios

MINDSET IS EVERYTHING

THE CHANCES ARE IF YOU ARE STRUGGLING TO LOSE WEIGHT THEN YOU NEED TO GET TO WORK ON YOUR MINDSET.

*Y*ou're scrolling through the jaw-dropping before/after pictures online and you have the burning need to know *exactly* what they've done to create a transformation like that. Watching everyone else around you looking amazing, showing up to events glowing, leaves you feeling like you've been left behind.

Weight Loss is not happening for you.

You may have even purchased products from websites or social media sellers promising you dramatic weight loss and results by doing very little than drinking tea, popping a herbal remedy or mixing up a juice each morning. We generally start looking these companies up and scrolling towards the businesses we would normally avoid who are taking advantage of when we're in a place of deepest despair and push us to take immediate action. You get hounded with emails, Facebook/Google ads all pointing you back to the website encouraging you to buy whilst your headspace is still the emotional state of desperation.

Welcome to the world of social media marketing , facebook ads and false before and after photos all thriving from women drowning in their low self-esteem.

The bottom line is regardless of how much you spend on these products and plans, you already know deep down that none of it really works. You have just had enough. Tired of trying, tired of looking in the mirror, desperate to change and willing to do anything or everything to get your *old body* back.

The best thing about this book is you have already tried to lose weight with every method that's been marketed to you so we can skip all the parts where I tell you they don't work and are a load of BS. We can both mutually agree that you have been marketed too by these companies based on your demolished body confidence, you wasted your hard-earned money and invested your time in all the wrong places.

Because of this mutual understanding between us, we can begin our work together to create a body that not only looks good but a body that feels good to be in.

How? By changing the way, you think.

This one simple exercise will really determine where your headspace is at, so let us try it for a moment...

You are late for the school run, barely brushed your hair and across the school yard coming towards you is Claire. Claire from your school days who you have not seen in ten years and now here she is skipping across the yard with her three kids and a figure-hugging activewear. As she approaches you beaming that she has recognised you, you look her up and down and realise she has not aged one bit. Her body is that of a model - toned, she has the perfect figure, and her face is glowing. You however want to hide. Your unbrushed hair and unmatched tracksuit makes you feel inept. She looks so so good and after hearing she has had three kids and still looks that hot you begin to wish the school yard would swallow you up.

So now I want you to evaluate your headspace the moment you get home from the school run. Do you:

- Stare in the mirror for ten minutes cursing out every single part of your body?
- Decide that from Monday you are eating carrot sticks only?
- Start googling, "fast weight loss methods"?
- Cry into a family sized chocolate bar that some girls are so lucky?
- Message your bestie and tell her all about that bitch Claire?

Now if you do any of the above or have been guilty of similar situations in the past it is time to recognise that these are all mindset issues. Whether it is driven from low self-esteem, body confidence issues, negative self-talk or lack of self-worth we are going to address them *all* in this book. So that by the time you have finished reading this book your reaction to Claire will be simply "nada". Because you will love your body the exact same way Claire does, if not even more so, because the value of working on your mindset is beyond any sweaty gym session can provide.

This book is not about who can lose the most weight, in fact this book is for any woman who has ever had issues with loving the body they are in. You may wish to lose 7lbs or 70lbs, but this is irrelevant in this book as I will focus on the issues that have created this mindset of needing to lose weight and guide you on a natural approach to healthy living which in turn will see the pounds fall off and allow you to step into a body you love every morning.

All I need from you is to be open to the activities I set you in this book and work on them daily for the next 90 days. I've even made it easy for you by including a free work-book you can download from the website www.mindfitmindset.com This workbook will allow you complete the activities in each chapter and reflect on how each mindset directly relates to the struggles you are having around your own body image and self-talk.

This book is by far the smallest investment you have made on changing your body but will in turn will bring you the greatest results. Why? Because it is written by someone who, like you, has chased faddy diets, splurged on diet pills and pined over photos of the body that once upon a time they looked hot in. I dedicate every day to helping women create a body they love by prioritising the mindset over the method. The method becomes minor once you nail the mindset needed to create phenomenal results.

So what is Mindfit Mindset™ and how will it work for you personally? Mindfit is all about focusing on the direct mindsets that are preventing you from creating a body you love. It captures the beliefs formed from childhood, past experiences and your environment that has shaped your body image over the last twenty years and has led you to feeling incapable of falling in love with your body. In this book we will overcome your limiting beliefs one by one and create an unbreakable mindset that will ultimately lead you to create a body you love with ease. Mindfit Mindset™ is endorsed by medical professionals, shared by fitness professionals globally and has helped accelerate weight loss in hundreds of women worldwide.

Spending time working on your mindset is by no way saying that you are at fault or that you are not doing it right. It is a form of self-development and growth. Mindset is all about how you perceive situations and whether you see obstruction as a barrier or an opportunity to learn. Many parts of this book will surprise you as you identify your own personal blocks to weight loss and how very simple changes can take you from yo-yo dieting to really experiencing the body transformation you've longed for.

Let us get acquainted, I'm Jenna, mum of five, Weight Loss Expert and Positive Psychology Practitioner. I am a Level four Obesity and Diabetes Specialist and help women ditch faddy diets for good and create a body they love by training their strongest muscle first - their mind! As a Positive Psychology Practitioner, I understand the power of connecting mindset with action to gain phenomenal results and that is what I want for every woman who reads this book.

Since having five children I am now two stones lighter and the healthiest I have ever been. The journey of hating my body and getting re-focused on me was a difficult one and as an experienced Life Coach for over twelve years it is a mindset process that I found was not overly documented or accessible. Having access to some of the best Life Coaches and Therapists has taught me the exact method needed for creating a body you love and I pride myself on sharing every battle I faced personally and the exact methods used to overcome them.

General mindset training is difficult to interpret to weight loss and body image so I hope you find this book useful, and I would love to hear your "aha" moments and transformations in my DMs. Remember we are creating the best version of you and therefore no one person will experience this book the same way. This is because our mindset is formed around our cultural, social and learned experiences and we all create barriers to prevent us from achieving our goals in different ways.

You may well find this new version of you showing up in other areas of your life embracing new opportunities and desires - you were warned! This happened with one of my amazing clients Jade. She started working with me with the primary goal being weight loss (1.5 stones to be precise) and felt like after having kids she really had not prioritised her health and wellbeing as much as she should. Upon recognising the need for a full body transformation, we began working on all the fixed beliefs she had formed about her body and the attitudes she had towards exercise. The most she had ever lost during previous weight loss attempts was 4lbs but by including Mindfit Mindset™ work she accelerated that weight loss to hit her goal 1.5 stone in just twelve weeks. But let me share the best bit of this transformation - she is beyond in love with her body. For the first time in seven years, she feels happy when she looks in the mirror, motivated to continue with exercising and has seen her mental health and wellbeing reach its highest ever levels. That for me is the secret formula of mindset working its way from the inside out.

I will be sharing exactly how to get these results for yourself at home without training at the gym seven days a week, depriving yourself from all your favourite foods and crying every time you weigh yourself. This is Mindfit Mindset™.

To help teach you the details of how to create this mindset at home I have structured this book in the format of affirmations that you need to be committed to implementing when losing weight and creating your own body transformation. Some will require more implementation than others but nonetheless it is important to read each chapter and take notes on where these mindsets are showing up for you and document your thoughts in the downloadable workbook. Acknowledgement of your mindset blocks and taking inspired action and changes based on this book will accelerate your weight loss in ways you have never experienced.

Will you simply read this book and lose a stone? No. But put in the actionable steps from this book into your everyday life and you will see noticeable changes both physically and mentally from the offset and by twelve weeks of using this book alongside a basic exercise and healthy eating regime you will become a whole improved version of what you once were.

The main point you need to know about this book is that just adapting your mindset will not allow you to lose weight, however what it will do is enable you to take the inspired action needed and be more effective and consistent thus making the weight loss journey more enjoyable and positive experience. This book is perfect for aligning your dream body with the action you are taking, to see the realm of opportunity. No more looking in the mirror longing for what once was, this book is about creating a newer, better version of you. It is time for us to get started, I don't know about you, but I cannot wait!

I AM A WORTHY OF A BODY I LOVE.

VISUALISE YOUR SUCCESS AND THEN TAKE INSPIRED ACTION.

*S*elf-worth is one of the key drivers when it comes to weight loss and creating a healthy lifestyle. I want to start by carrying out a self-evaluation to discover if you are meeting the basic needs for your psychological wellbeing and from there we can begin to build on your self-worth. I want you to answer the following two questions honestly and openly in your journal or using the workbook available on www.mindfitmindset.com

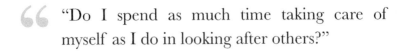

"Do I spend as much time taking care of myself as I do in looking after others?"

This first question centres around self-care and where you see yourself in the priority list. This 'so-called' priority list, which is created by you, needs re-evaluating and making relevant changes before we can even step foot in the gym or beginning a weight loss plan. When we hear the word 'self-care' it is often perceived as being selfish and self-centred, both traits we are inherently aiming to stay away from.

Therefore, self-care requires us to negotiate within ourselves daily whether in fact the scheduled activities we have planned are really required. For example, have you ever changed your plans to head to the gym the minute you realise your child has homework due the next day, your best friend calls you for a natter and you lose 30 minutes of your gym session, the burst pipe at home requires you to stay at home today instead of work out? We'll talk about self-sabotage in the next chapter but what I want you to consider is how many things do you allow to jump the queue in your priority list and who do you allow to jump the queue.

Complete this in the workbook and really start to recognise whether these do in fact take priority or whether you allow them to do so in avoidance of making yourself a priority. Can you make both situations a priority? – absolutely! The key to self-worth is always keeping you on that priority list and recognising that you are deserving of having goals and making them a must-do in your schedule.

As a crazy busy mum of five, I recognised self-care as being the saviour tool that would allow me to get through the struggle of giving birth to five children in five years. That is my fun fact by the way, I have done well not to mention it up until this point in the book, but my children are my biggest life achievement and the fact I raised them all independently is a miracle within itself. However, this journey was over-whelming I just could not fathom where I fit into my own priority list. I am not talking about anxiety about not having time for my nails or eyelash appointments. These things are superficial and have no place in self-worth. I had anxiety around my health. My biggest fear has and probably always will be, is who would take care of my children if I were not around or able. We can't control what is written for us, but we can give ourselves a healthy lifestyle, fuel our bodies with nutritious food and aim to be as healthy as possible. This includes good quality sleep, sufficient energy levels and keeping our wellbeing tank full. When you start to invest in self-care you have a real understanding that this relates to your health and wellbeing and selfishness does not come into it.

Self-care looks different to everyone and that is why it is important that you come up with your own version. Take out your workbook and create a list of your current self-care regime and how you can step it up a notch. My routine includes a bi-weekly lunch or coffee out with friends, aromatherapy massage once a month, three sessions in the gym weekly, three litres of water daily, home-cooked food, fifteen minutes each evening reading a book. These things all support me with handling the busy routines and endless piles of washing as I know that I have time put aside for me.

By creating your own list of self-care must do activities will allow you to enter the priority list therefore creating higher levels of wellbeing and motivation. In positive psychology optimal wellbeing is described as 'flourishing'.

The second question we need to discuss is around your connection to your body and your overall levels of happiness.

 "Is my weight defining my happiness?"

You want to say no – don't you? But the truth is in reality many women wanting to lose weight directly equate the number of the scales to how happy they feel about their body. The more you understand the meaning of happiness and how it derives the more you understand the connection between mindset, happiness and your physical being i.e. your weight. This is the research carried out by my area of study, Positive Psychology.

If you answered "Yes" straight away, then I applaud you for being so honest and I can put my hand on heart and say this book will help to separate the two and understand the thoughts that are leading you to that conclusion.

I want to give you a brief introduction to my area of specialism, Positive Psychology, which is often defined as the science of happiness and wellbeing. One of the founders of the movement, Martin Seligman, defines happiness as

"A state of wellbeing or contentment, a pleasurable or satisfying experience."

I've studied Positive Psychology for over ten years and I'm confident in defining the relationship between happiness and weight loss as crucial when it comes to creating a body you love.

In order to separate the two, you need to understand what influences your happiness and how much control you have over it. Positive Psychologist Sonja Lyubomirsky concludes following extensive research that our happiness is determined by three different factors: our genes, our circumstances and our intentional activity. You may be surprised to learn that 50% of our happiness is determined by our genetics and therefore is set and cannot be influenced. Our circumstances define just 10% of our wellbeing and the remaining 40% we have autonomy over is the intentional activity.

So when we think about our wellbeing and how our physical body is causing an impact knowing that we have 40% control of over how we feel about body should instil you with confidence that in fact we do have the ability to change your body from the inside out by carrying out intentional activity to reprogram our mindset and our thoughts. This book is going to give you plenty of tools to start that work and it's for that reason each chapter centres around a new affirmation that we are subconsciously creating in your mind.

Another area to point out in the study of happiness is that circumstances really don't have much impact on your well-being so it would be true to say that those excuses and limiting beliefs preventing you from doing and being out there and getting the body you love are purely that "excuses". We will cover limiting beliefs and self-sabotage later in the book.

If you answered "Yes" to allowing your weight to define your happiness, then this book will be the tool you need to change that around. In your workbook or your journal I want to write down specifically what areas of your body make you unhappy and/or what circumstances influence this. Your list can be short or long but take time in really figuring out where you are relating the two. Once you've identified this list, I want you to refer to the three elements of happiness and mark whether these thoughts are controlled by genetics, circumstances or intentional activity.

To give you an example my client Lynda used to serve in the police and had a very athletic body build. She linked her happiness to her weight by always referring to herself as big boned and chunky. She hated the way she looked based on these two statements. She acknowledged the place that genetics played however it was her limited beliefs around her body type and frame that prevented her from intentional activity to help her change. Whenever she got ready for an evening out, she would refer to herself as the less glamorous one, or wear all black to blend in or shun off any compliments. These behaviours all links to the psychology of how you perceive your body to be and I can't wait to share with you all the tools you can use to overcome these repeated behaviours.

Self-care is being overly used lately in the media and can be manipulated into making you believe it is selfish and based purely on aesthetics like getting your nails done etc. However, I like to define Self Care as this;

 "Preserving your health and happiness"

So therefore reading fifteen minutes every evening, enjoying a bubble bath, working out and cooking all form part of my self-care routine. Your self-care should be daily and done by you for you. Nobody else is responsible for your self-care and it will not work if you are waiting or relying on someone else for this to be a reality. I want you to really take note of this point.

One of my favourite ways to prioritise self-care is by having a structured morning and night time routine. Both are only 30 minutes and I'm going to share them with you below, but this is why it helps. Your morning routine helps set the intention for the day and clears any negative thoughts which may impact your start to the day. For example have you ever rolled over in bed, picked up your phone and seen that Z-list celebrity post yet another bikini shot just three weeks after giving birth and it's thrown your whole mood off. This is an extreme example but you get the point. What you look at on your phone in the morning can often define your mood therefore phones are off limits in my house until 8.30am when my workday is about to begin.

This also applies in the evening how you fall asleep affects your quality of sleep and levels of anxiety, wellbeing, and mood. Therefore, preserving that time before you go to sleep will allow you to wake up feeling refreshed and ready to take on the day. If you've never tried this before I want you to carve out a 30-60min routine for your morning and evening routine and try it out for a full seven days. I promise you once you've tried this you will never go back. I've included my routine below but feel free to put in any additions of your own.

(06:00 – 06:30)

WAKE

SKINCARE

AFFIRMATIONS AND GRATTITUDE Read all three whilst looking at my vision board

PRAY

10 MIN RUN on the treadmill

(09:00)

CHECK DIARY for the day, review priorities, reply to any clients or overnight emails

(21:30 – 22:00)

LIGHT CANDLE

GRATTITUDE JOURNAL

SKINCARE ROUTINE

PJS ON

15 MIN READ BOOK

SLEEP

I literally do not deviate from this routine, however the times can change during summer I start my day at 05:30 instead but the routine itself is non-negotiable. Try it and let me know how you get on.

Key Learnings from this chapter.

- Self Care is NOT Selfish.
- Self-Care routines are all about preserving your health and happiness.
- Happiness is determined by our genes, our circumstances and our intentional activity.

I AM CAPABLE... AND SOME!

PROCRASTINATION IS BY FAR THE WORST FORM OF SELF-SABOTAGE

This affirmation is the one we all struggle to own for more than a few weeks. If you have ever started to lose weight, eat healthy or begin an exercise regime and it's destined that you will inevitably give up then you will know what I'm talking about. Self-sabotage - aka messing it up for yourself even though you were doing well. See if either of these sounds like you:

-You're careful for a while, lose some weight, and improve your fitness... then gradually revert back to your old ways.

Or

-You know exactly what to do, but can't seem to do it. You feel like you could write a diet book with everything you know about weight loss. But you don't act on it.

The truth is, there's a huge difference between knowing what to do and actually doing it. It's easy to hop from one diet to the next without ever sticking with anything. Success (or lack thereof) comes down to our mindset, psychology, and habits.

No diet that is solely based on the food you eat will help you figure out why you gained weight in the first place. A diet won't fix emotional, mindless, stress-induced eating, and it won't fix habitual, compulsive binge-eating. Basically, a diet won't get to the root cause of why you overeat.

People often think a fear of failure is holding them back. I frequently hear, "I don't want this to be yet another failed attempt." But surprisingly, it's a fear of success that holds people back the most.

Why would you be scared of success? Well, if you're successful, any number of fears could be realised. For instance, you won't have food as a way to temporarily escape or quiet your mind at work or home. Or you'll have to deal with uncomfortable feelings such as self-doubt, regret, disappointment, or fear (because you're not suppressing them with food).

Maybe you'll lose the "Once I lose the weight I will finally…" safety blanket that protects you from taking action on an intimidating (but ultimately rewarding) prospect.

These are real psychological roadblocks, but nothing that can't be overcome. To break from a pattern of self-sabotage, you need to get to the root of why you're sabotaging yourself. Ask yourself this question.

Why would I be worse off when I lose weight?

This question helps address deep rooted mindset blocks that come to life which you have never previously acknowledged. I've had clients realise they thought they'd no longer be able to enjoy food, they weren't sure how they would enjoy a movie night with their partner, they thought they'd miss out on girls' nights out. The key to addressing these hidden blocks is to flip the question over and ask yourself,

Why would I be better off when I lose weight?

Write out the list and then reframe the mindset blocks you identified in the previous exercise for example:

66 "I will enjoy healthier foods and the options are endless."

66 "Me and partner can plan endless date nights and adventures."

66 "I can't wait to go out with the girls looking fabulous."

Add these to your list of Whys and keep this list to hand to re-motivate you when needed.

One of my clients, Saima, used to struggle with starting at the gym and then ending a few weeks later. She'd then message me to start again and the cycle continued for months until one day she asked me, "What is wrong with me? I can't stick to anything."

My response was you follow the, *Shit Cycle* and not the, *Glamfit Cycle.* Let me explain and please drop me a DM if this part of the book screams your name because the *Shit Cycle* is the biggest form of self-sabotage going and allows you to continue to fall off plan and destroy your chances of creating a body you love.

The Step-by-Step Shit Cycle

1. You're looking in the mirror depressed by what you see in the reflection.
2. You sign up to the next weight loss programme that catches your eye with a screen full of before and after pictures.
3. You restrict yourself painfully from food and hammer the gym as hard as you can to lose as much as you can as fast as you can.
4. CRASH – you eat a takeout, followed by a family sized chocolate bar.
5. You start again on Monday and tell yourself you're "Back on it".
6. You jump on the scales after two weeks of torture only to release you've lost a pound.

7. You decide that your method sucks and can't continue so you decide to park it up for a few weeks.

8. SELF-SABOTAGE happens and you go back to step 1.

Here's the worst thing about the *Shit Cycle* you start with feeling like shit, you feel like shit whilst you're doing it and it ends with you feeling like shit. Excuse the excessive swearing here but you get my gist it all revolves around negative feelings and the only positive part of the experience is when you weigh in and see that you've lost a pound or two. It's completely uninspiring and it's not surprising that you don't get any real results. Now see below the *GlamFIT cycle* which I use with my body transformation clients who on average lose 20lbs in my twelve week intensive studio program.

 ## The Step-by-Step GlamFIT "Plan to Glam"

1. You're inspired to take action by surrounding yourself with positive influence and healthy women.

2. You create a robust plan that you improve on every four weeks. You make it simple, do-able and allow for progression.

3. You start with a basic fitness and nutrition regime, monitoring step count, writing down your eating

habits. The more you understand your routine the easier it is to change.

4. You include Daily mindset work surrounded with affirmations, mindset exercises and being accountable to your plan on a daily basis.

5. Each week you carry out a "Non-critical Evaluation" (See Chapter 4 for more details) allowing you step up week on week and acknowledge all the changes you are making for the better and ditching the not so good habits.

6. You reward yourself with self-care treats for each week you keep going. Think facials, massages, new skincare etc. Rewarding yourself with treats that support your end goal whilst following your programme keeps your self-worth high and avoids treating yourself with a doughnut or some other excessively sugary snack. One word – Counter Productive!

7. Your body begins to adapt to your new lifestyle and you notice your mood lightening, your energy levels increasing and begin to feel more positive about the changes you're making.

8. You weigh in after four weeks acknowledging all the progress steps made and celebrate your win on the scale with yet again some more self-care. Back to step 1.

Here's the difference with this cycle, you are celebrating every win, you are in a positive mindset daily, your focus is not on the scales, you allow four weeks for your body to take shape and more importantly you stay focussed on the goal in sight. Because let's face it weight loss doesn't bring quick wins it takes time so leaning towards a lifestyle change and not a quick fix is one of the ways to not burn out from going in too hard too soon.

So now I've got you motivated I need to share with you my biggest loss, Rizwana. 54kg down and still losing weekly purely by following the *Glamfit cycle*. She remains dedicated and patient with her weight loss because she accepts it's a lifestyle and works on improving week on week. Every week for the last 18months Rizwana has improved. The secret of winning is understanding what doesn't work for you and replacing it with a positive changes and new habits. When you're still losing weight by month 18 then it proves that this mindset focussed cycle is well worth your time and dedication.

So how do you stay motivated and inspired when your mind is telling you otherwise?

Self-talk allows many of us to convince ourselves that we don't need to continue any further, that circumstances won't allow it or that we shouldn't have started in the first place. It works against the affirmation in this chapter "I am capable" and does everything to convince you that you are exactly the opposite of capable. I want to address two types of self-talk in this chapter which are projected to the forefront of your weight loss journey. The first one relates to your "Physical" appearance and the second one is "Emotional" and targets your character strengths.

Let's start with the first type of self-talk "Physical" as you are probably familiar with the type of self-talk that arrives when you look in the mirror. You're looking forward to an event where all your girlfriends will be present, and you've finished applying your makeup and stand up to look in the mirror. The self-talk begins, "You look like a mess." "Your stomach looks a state." "Ugly." and I'm guessing a whole lot worse. It ruins your mood before you leave the house and sometimes affects your confidence for the rest of the evening. This kind of self-talk would be heartbreaking if you were to say it out loud to your best friend when they'd just got ready for a night out. But you deem it acceptable to say it to yourself.

This physical self-talk is often what gets women started on their weight loss plans and diets but the self-talk itself doesn't go away - it gets worse. "You look like a state trying to run on the treadmill." "You fat cow - don't eat that!" "No wonder you're fat you can't exercise to save your life." And it's for this reason that understanding your motivation for wanting to lose weight really needs figuring out before you get started. Ask yourself.

What is the reason for me wanting to lose weight?

Come up with at least five reasons that come from a place of positivity and excitement for the future. This helps you uncover your motivations and it's important to document these to refer back to when you start to feel low. Everyone's motivation is completely different and can relate to health, energy, relief of aches and pains, improve sleep, or boost wellbeing levels. It is important to understand that everyone's motivation is different when you are comparing yourself to "Laura" in the gym who in your opinion has no reason to be there and is running on the treadmill purely just to highlight she's better than everyone else. She does have a reason to be there - you just don't know it. Every person's "why" is different.

Now you've created your list of motivations, you have a solid case of "whys" to refer back too. If you refer back to a motivation that says, "I want to look hot at my sister's wedding." this is more likely to fuel you with positive motivation to stay on track. Alternatively, if you refer back to your negative self-talk which stems from, "You look a hot mess." chances are this will result in self-sabotage and cause you to eat a family sized chocolate bar… it happens. Being aware of your self-talk can be overcome by replacing the negative self-talk with the positive motivations you create in this chapter. Pin them to the biscuit cupboard if you need to…. this really works.

I'll never forget when I looked at my body for the first time after giving birth. No one had prepared me for the way I would feel after carrying a baby for nine months. It was all focussed on how miraculous our bodies were for bringing this beautiful life into this world. I get it. No, I really get it. It's amazing what our body is capable of. But did anyone bother to tell me my stomach would have excess vomit-inducing skin, my 'down below' would be torn to bits and I would never be able to hold my urine the same again? I felt awful. I remember staring at my body and knowing exactly why women, 'let themselves go' after giving birth. A stone of extra weight on the scale, teamed with exhaustion, the after effects of childbirth are real. The negative self-talk I used about my body became harsher and harsher.

I began researching the words which have probably been googled thousands of times.

"Get my body back after giving birth."

"Quickest way to lose baby weight."

"Best diet for losing pregnancy weight."

However, the support I needed was much more psychological and one I'll cover more in this book and that is the way we frame our situations and fail to keep an open mind to the possibilities around us. The truth is it doesn't matter if you had your baby six months ago or six years ago if you hate your body you will inevitably stay the same.

The second type of self-talk is 'emotional' and directly links to a lack of self-belief and learned behaviours. Emotional self-talk is the soul-destroying thing you say to yourself when attempting something new or attempting to implement change. You remove the 'Anything is possible' mantra and replace it with everything you cannot do and link it to previous scenarios to act as 'evidence' as to why you are about to mess this whole thing up.

Emotional self-talk works against your character key strengths so an important way to overcome this talk is to acknowledge your strengths out loud, through journaling and through positive affirmations. There are many personality strength tests available online that will help you with this task but I find a list of five to ten strengths will be enough to overcome emotional self-talk.

To give you an example of how character strengths can support you I will share with you a revelation I had personally when discovering my own. I have this incredible ability to make light of every dull situation by laughing and turning it into humour. I didn't realise this strength until I spoke to a few family members and my bestie so I started to read further into it from a positive psychology perspective. It turns out people who laugh more have stronger immune systems and are less stressed than those who don't due to hormone balances. Whenever I experience negative self-talk I decide to laugh about it and share it with someone close and laugh about it together. Yes I sound bonkers and my thoughts are far-fetched but at least I can now identify it as a strength!

Identify your strengths and create affirmations based around your strengths. *I am capable. I am worthy of an amazing body, I am entitled to invest time looking after me.* It's for this reason the whole premise of this book is written with affirmations so you can truly embody each statement, understand your mindset and work towards your goals in a way you never have before. Once you begin to embody these affirmations the true Mindfit Mindset begins.

Key Learnings from this chapter

- Overcome self-sabotage by understanding your mindset blocks and reframing them.
- Kill of negative self-talk by understanding your *true* motivation.
- Identify your character strengths to overpower emotional self-talk.

I ALWAYS HAVE TIME FOR ME

PROCRASTINATION IS BY FAR THE WORST
FORM OF SELF-SABOTAGE

The 'I don't have time to exercise' excuse has always worn pretty thin with me and despite that it is still the most common reason only 1 in 3 people in the UK exercise. Let's stay friends and let me explain my point. You probably know by now that I had five kids in five years, run my household independently and run a business AND still manage to keep self-care a priority. That is the key word - priority. Not time. Not commitment. Priority.

Time has always been something I wish I had more of therefore planning my day is an essential part in making sure I get everything done. The most effective method for me managing the kids, business and household is to block time out for certain tasks. For example, my morning routine is completed between 6am and 7am therefore I am free at 7am to concentrate purely on getting the kids up and dressed, breakfast and getting them out of the house at 8.30am.

In the evenings I use an hour of work on my business growth twice a week. I schedule the time blocks even the 'time with friends' to ensure my week runs as smoothly as it can, therefore maintaining my wellness levels.

I wanted to discuss my personal reasons why I see being healthy as such a priority and hope that will inspire you to add your health to your priority list as this certainly overcomes any scheduling or 'time-poor' issues I often hear about. I exercise for both my physical health but more so my mental health. I've suffered from anxiety for over ten years since moving out of my parents' home at the young age of seventeen and having to deal with 'adult' issues before I was emotionally ready. Exercise was my saviour. Whenever I exercised the release of daily endorphins kept me pumped for the day ahead and were partly the reason how at just the age of seventeen, I juggled a full time job and full time college. It was always a miracle to me how I still managed to achieve A Grades all whilst sleeping on a mattress in a dirty flat, but I wholeheartedly put that down to me using exercise as an outlet for my anxiety.

Since then, I have only stopped exercising when heavily pregnant and surprise surprise that's when my anxiety went through the roof. The minute I began exercising postpartum it returns to a normal non-medicated state. I by no means compromise my mental health and therefore for me staying physically and mentally healthy allows me to show up as the best version of me! The one here… writing this book. My health is wealth and therefore it is my priority.

With the number of options available to introduce health and wellbeing into your life it now doesn't require you to even leave your home, you can exercise from home, follow online nutrition plans, get coached by the best weight loss coaches - feel free to add my name right here. You get my point it's now easier than ever to get started on your journey.

So let's work out what self-care means to you. It doesn't have to be expensive facials, high end products or blowing your earnings on new clothes. Self-care for me is very simple which is why I always have time to include it in my schedule. Long soaks in the bath, fifteen minutes reading every day, journaling, meeting up weekly with friends, thirty minutes exercise all form part of my non-negotiable self-care routine. My priorities.

To help you I suggest forming your own version of priorities, ignore the day to day as that will go on regardless and create a list of non-negotiable self-care rituals that you will complete as a priority. This will directly improve your health and wellness levels and time no longer becomes a factor. If you completed the task in the last chapter you will have already begun to work on this.

So having the perfect routine all sounds well and good but you're probably wondering what happens when sh*t hits the fan! And it does quite regularly in my house and can turn into chaos very quickly. In those moments I shelve everything I'm doing and deal with the situation in hand. I then reschedule my priorities back into my diary and remove the ones further down the list that won't impact my health and wellbeing i.e. meeting with friends, browsing social media, speaking on the phone for an hour. And just about I can manage to keep my health and well-being still at the forefront of what I do.

Without a doubt there will be times when exercise won't be an option for example when a relative is extremely ill or someone passes away. That is not the time to be in the gym but make sure this is an extreme circumstance rather than an 'excuse'. I run my clients on this rule 'Excuses must be rescheduled!' for whenever my clients message me last minute.

So now we have established we have the time, it is time to create goals that will set you up for winning and I want to share my three-part formula for goal setting that I use on my own personal training clients and that as a result led me to design the number one best-selling planner on Etsy – *Plan to Glam*. This goal-setting method has already been used by over 1000 women in the UK and the planner allows them to stay accountable to this exact method. My client Anna is now on her third planner and has lost over six stones – wow! She attributes the success to the accountability and visualisation method used to write the plan. I've created a printable version of the plan in the workbook which you can complete as you read this chapter. I'd recommend spending at least sixty minutes on creating the plan so you know you've nailed all three steps.

Planning is so important when it comes to creating a body you love, it allows you to focus on making your goals a reality and achieving milestones you previously believed weren't possible. I want to use this chapter to introduce to you one of the major theories studied in Positive Psychology and that is the PERMA theory of wellbeing. It's believed that should one include all elements of the PERMA model into each action then you would flourish and thrive in everything you are doing. I've included the PERMA model into my own GlamFIT Planner and really want to break down the theory of this in this chapter. I want to start by giving you a brief introduction to each element of the PERMA model and how we can apply this to weight loss.

P – POSITIVE EMOTION

The route to optimal living is hedonic – aiming to increase positive emotion in our life to its maximum. Within its limits we create positive emotion around our past experiences (Through gratitude, learning and forgiveness techniques) and we cultivate positive emotion around the future (hope, optimism, visualisations etc) we have the winning formula in creating our best life. And let's face it that's what we are all aiming for. Optimal living, optimal wellbeing, and happiness.

Therefore, understanding the role of positive emotion when referring to weight loss is essential. When looking at our own experiences of weight loss it's important to acknowledge our previous attempts i.e., what went well and what didn't and remove the negative believes we have around what we are and aren't capable of when creating our bodies. Surrounding our new experience of weight loss with positive emotions will be the difference between it being successful or failing miserably.

To help support our positive emotions for the future we need to visualise exactly the goal we are trying to achieve and become laser focused on what could be achieved with perseverance and focus.

E – ENGAGEMENT

Engagement is the experience of someone deploying their skills to a task that's been set which allows them to enjoy the experience a remain in 'flow' with the task in hand. The gratification you have by completing the task efficiently and effectively allows you to continue towards a goal with ease and enjoyment.

It's the engagement part of beginning a fitness or nutrition plan which is often short-lived when starting out on a weight loss goal. Most women find the whole process excruciating and hard-work so by creating a plan that's do-able and enjoyable is essential to the overall result.

R - RELATIONSHIPS

Connections to others and how we interact is essential to optimal wellbeing. Feeling like you belong when striving for a specific goal allows you to keep pushing through the lows and helps you celebrate the highs.

When working on a fitness and nutrition plan ensuring you have the correct support around you can be the difference between success and failure. It's for this reason women training in group programmes or recruit an accountability coach like myself to help push them towards their goals. Ultimately it matters who you are around when trying to lose weight whether that's in person or virtually. They need to inspire you and motivate you so choose them wisely.

M - MEANING

The purpose you attach to a specific task or result must be bigger than oneself in order for it to reach a level beyond what's been achieved before.

In terms of exercise the bigger goal of a healthier lifestyle supersedes the number of pounds lost on the scales. It's for this reason you'll see in a moment why I put so much emphasis on exploring the reasons 'Why' you want to lose weight. The better understanding you have of your reasoning will allow you further satisfaction with the result.

A – ACCOMPLISHMENT

Women pursue achievement, competence, success and mastery in everything from the workplace, homelife, hobbies, raising our children. It's important for us to be successful in what we set our minds too.

This is why many weight loss companies purely focus on the end result being a quantitative figure, usually the pounds lost on the scale. However, looking qualitative measures are equally important and still lead to the feeling of accomplishment, therefore one single measure is not enough when working on your weight loss plan.

Hopefully the above has given you a good insight into the theory I've researched when creating the Mindfit Mindset strategy for weight loss. So it might excite you to know the next part is creating the plan. I've included a section in the workbook you can use to complete your personalised plan or you purchase one of the *Plan to Glam* Planners through Etsy and begin your 90 day programme today.

Let's talk through the GlamFIT *Plan to Glam* which incorporates the PERMA Positive Psychology Model explained above.

Step 1 – Motivation (What's making you do this now?)

Motivation is all about understanding the key drivers in your reason for getting started. What has happened to bring you to the point where you need to make serious changes and take the needed action? Write down the reason you want to change now at this present moment in your workbook and then ask yourself why?

This simple psychological activity identifies the two types of motivation; Intrinsic or Extrinsic. Intrinsic motivation is led from inner self-development, mastery and fulfilling your purpose. Extrinsic motivation is lead from external factors such as circumstance, punishment, need to be accepted and desperation. Take a look back at your answer and have a look which category of motivation it fits.

Chances are your motivations are generally led from extrinsic factors and this is quite common when it comes to weight loss goals. However, by picking up this book as your guide to lose weight is a much more intrinsic motivation, meaning you care about the long-term results. It is for this reason I take the goal-setting level into two further levels deeper to ensure that you are not just driven by extrinsic motivation and aim for better results than you've ever achieved previously.

Step 2 – Dedication (How you plan to get from A to B)

This sections defines the exact action you are going to take to reach the end goal, broken down into four areas. The more specific you are with these areas the more successful you will be. I always recommend being realistic and looking to improve your plan every four weeks until you're working at your optimal level.

The first area focuses on improving your N.E.A.T (Non-exercise activity thermogenesis). This is basically the energy (kcals) you burn on a normal day through your daily activity. It doesn't involve exercise and focuses on your daily calorie expenditure. One of the most well-known ways to measure this is through your step count and I do highly recommend that if you don't monitor your step count now's the time to get started. Aim for 8000 a day if you're brand new to walking you can work your way up to 15000 a day adding on 500 every four weeks.

The second area is the physical activity, or workouts you are going to commit to. Workouts can be anything from a dance class, gym session, swimming or taking a walk. Either way make a commitment and ensure it's realistic to both your ability and timetable. The ideal starting point is two walks and two gym sessions but feel free to start with three sessions a week and increase it from there. Also remember that sessions don't need to be 60 minutes, you can choose 2 x 30min treadmill sessions and 2 x 45 minutes walks. Start with what you are able and look to level up every four weeks.

The third area under dedication is looking at nutrition. Now I've written a whole chapter on the psychology of healthy eating but all I ever expect my women to work on is three improvements that will support their end goal i.e. drink three litres of water, replace snacks with fruit etc. The key with nutrition is starting with basic improvements and look to improve week on week. Aiming for a perfectly nutritious week is hard even for the best of us so remove the pressure from yourself and keep your nutrition goals simple and achievable.

The fourth section is all about self-care, yes I know we've just covered this in the last chapter but adding self-care to your actual plan allows a reward every four weeks in return for the effort you're putting in. The positive rein-forcement you get from a 60min massage every four weeks is much more effective than scheduling a 'treat day' which is completely counter-intuitive for the work you are doing and the end goal. What is the point of working out all week and rewarding yourself with a doughnut – right? So, coming up with a list of treats which you decide is your way of showing yourself respect and honouring your self-worth. The theory behind this again relates to positive psychology and the

PERMA theory of being fulfilled by the plan you've created.

Step 3 – Inspiration (Connecting the why to the vision)

The secret of change is to focus all of your energy not on fighting the old but building the new.

The inspiration section of the plan is all about understanding the reason why we are doing it in the first place and connecting with positive emotions attached to that feeling. It's taking your motivation to the next level and allowing us to connect deeper to our vision of becoming a newer healthier happier you.

Positive emotion is created by visualising an experience before it happens, and weight loss works in the exact same way. Visualising yourself slim or wearing an outfit you've been wanting to get into is often one of the first things we think about when we begin a health kick.

So why is it so hard to keep this visualisation and turn it into reality?

Why is this not enough motivation for us?

Why do we give up after just a few weeks?

It's because we haven't connected deeply enough to the 'Inspiration' part of the plan and haven't developed a connection to the visual we want to create.

To do this, you need to find a calming, relaxing place at home where you can sit and really imagine what success is going to look like for you, bearing in mind that looks differently for everyone. Don't imagine a version of you that somebody else wants you look like, imagine how you would be once you hit your target goals and were on track for the body of your dreams.

Imagine:

What do you look like?

What clothes are you wearing?

How do your clothes fit?

How have you styled your hair?

Are you wearing makeup?

How do you look when you're going out with friends?

What would you be wearing if you were to go out for the evening?

Write down all of these in your journal and continually revisit this image of yourself daily upon waking and sleeping.

Next start to connect with how you now feel in yourself:

What emotions do you feel?

Has your confidence improved?

How do you react to a compliment?

How do you feel when you look in the mirror?

How do you friends/partner describe your look?

Allow all these positive emotions into your visualisation and connect with them as though they are already happening for you. I'll revisit visualisations again in the last chapter but this visual of the happier healthier you is going to be around until you become her so be prepared for me to refer to this visual throughout this book.

The last part of the visualisation is to look at what this newer, happier version of you can now do once you've achieved your goals:

How do you shop for clothes?

How do you now enter a room?

How do approach new people?

How are you around friends and family?

Think about everything that you'd created a restriction to doing because of your body confidence now being opened and record each and every one of these in your journal.

You've now completed your *Plan to Glam* and to stay on track you need to revisit these goals daily and more importantly connect to your visualisation each and every morning. This plan is unlike any plan you've created before and that's because it's created using the PERMA theory described above.

You are now all set to begin using this plan to begin your journey. The next part of this book will now support you in taking your visualisation into reality so you will never need to repeat another faddy diet EVER again. The excitement you feel now you know where you're heading and exactly how you are going to get there is what drives me in wanting to help so many more women reach their goals. The next part of this book is going to take you through creating your new mindset – Mindfit, and the actions you will need to take to reach the finish line.

Key learnings from this chapter

- Health is wealth
- Positive emotions drive results
- Plan to Glam

ANYTHING IS POSSIBLE

SHE BELIEVED SHE COULD, SO SHE DID

We are brought up to believe and are constantly reminded by everyone that, 'we can't have it all' and that some people are just lucky. We are taught that if we are successful in one aspect of life, we won't be thriving in another. What I love about positive psychology is that it teaches us that we can be fulfilled in all areas of wellbeing in our life and that in fact anything IS possible.

Did you ever hear,

"They have money, but they won't find happiness."

"She may look amazing, but she struggles to find love."

"She spends lot of time looking after herself, but she doesn't have friends."?

It's a common theory in our society to believe that to be successful in all aspects of life is near impossible. Many people apply this exact same theory to weight loss even if they do it subconsciously. We place two comparable aspects of someone's life and attribute that to their success.

> "She's only slim because she has the time to spend in the gym."

> *"She's no time to look good because she's so career focused."*

> *"She's newly found love she's not watching her weight."*

This chapter is all about unlocking the possibilities and looking at how you can have it all without any limitations.

Mindfit Mindset centres around the belief that all of your goals can be achieved and your success is not limited to any external factors. One of the biggest barriers to weight loss often centres around fixed beliefs that have been formed from a young age, developed throughout our teens and then cemented through our experiences as an adult. Some of these fixed beliefs centre specifically around our body image, but the deeper fixed beliefs around our ability levels and factors of live are the REAL barriers that are preventing our success when it comes to weight loss. I'm going to run through these fixed beliefs below and give you examples of how it's held my clients back specifically but consider how each and every one of the below beliefs may be affecting you on your journey to a healthier, happier you.

Fixed beliefs begin in the conscious mind and are brought about by learned experiences. I often see in clients whose end goals are weight loss, that they don't actually believe that they will get results. They may sign up to a programme *wanting* results but don't truly believe that they are capable of achieving the results. This is due to the fixed beliefs they already have around weight loss.

Fixed Belief – It won't happen for me.

Halima has been trying to lose weight since the age 16 when she was told by her mum that in order to get married she would have to sort out her weight problem. She had been to every gym in the local area and had been exercising for the four years. Her weight had fluctuated by about half a stone loss but then usually regained within a month or two and this pattern had continued over the four years.

She came to me in a state of exhaustion. She told me she worked really hard in the gym three times a week and ate well 80% of the time. She believed that she was genetically meant to always be big and there weren't many options available to her. This fixed belief was holding her back so much she genuinely believed that she had tried everything.

I took her through the *Plan to Glam* and we begun that week. Once we'd discussed all the possible things, we could change about her lifestyle she began to believe that change was possible. Within a month she'd lost a stone.

Fixed beliefs are what you believe to be absolute certain and truthful. Once these are formed your subconscious mind beliefs these to be true and brings them to reality. These beliefs are often limited meaning we allow no room for us to allow for a growth mindset. With limited beliefs you tend to lean towards the negative allowing no room for these thoughts and opinions to be changed.

Limiting beliefs are often formed in childhood it's also likely that they are inherited from your family and culture. Your parents' beliefs about life are often instilled into you from a young age. Education also plays a major role, whether you are learning from family, teachers, or friends they all have an impact on what you adopt as truth. This is because they're both in a position of authority and are constantly sharing information, ideas, and beliefs about how the world works. The third way limiting beliefs are formed is through experiences in life. Negative experiences help you draw conclusions on how life is and therefore how it will continue to play out for you.

When looking at limiting beliefs when talking about weight loss many beliefs have been formed through negative experiences. For example, were you bullied as a child for being overweight? Have you tried and failed repeatedly? Have you been under pressure to lose weight from others? These experiences all form limiting beliefs about what you *feel* you are capable of achieving.

Task – Ask yourself what you believe to be true about your body and what do you believe to be true about weight loss.

Write them all down however trivial you know them to be, if that's what your mind believes then the first step is to acknowledge it.

Once you've written them down, work out how this believe was formed

Then create a counter statement challenging that belief.

Write that in your diary and remind yourself daily.

Limiting beliefs affect the connection between your plan and your goals. Under the PERMA in positive psychology, it affects the following areas.

P – POSITIVE EMOTION

As limiting beliefs are often negative statements it works against the mindset of *can do* and pulls you towards the attitude of *cannot*. By implementing a growth mindset, you can begin to open yourself up to new ideas and ways of creating the body you desire.

E – ENGAGEMENT

Limiting Beliefs don't allow you bring the plan you've created to fruition because your subconscious mind believes that it is not physically capable of completing the task given. In order to bring any goal or ambition to life you have to be engaged in the emotions attached to that plan. Therefore it's important to work on eliminating the beliefs on a daily basis and continually visualising your success.

R – RELATIONSHIPS

Let's talk about other people's opinions on your weight loss and how debilitating it can really be for someone to be constantly giving their two pence worth about what you should and shouldn't be doing. Their own limited beliefs around weight loss are forced upon you it's important you recognise this and learn how to zone out when they are offering their advice. This is relatively easy to do when you're used to hearing them on repeat.

Certain family members or spouses may have their own limited beliefs around your capability and chance of success. These limiting beliefs can be catastrophic on your weight loss journey, so these issues need to be addressed form the outset. A strong word with the individual usually suffices. Explain to them the impact of them doubting you constantly and seek support and accountability from someone you trust.

M – MEANING

Attaching a meaning to your weight loss journey really helps when overcoming limiting beliefs. If you believe that you're doing something, for a greater cause (i.e. exercising for your health) you are less likely to form beliefs around what you can and can't achieve. When forming new beliefs around your goals focus on what you **can** do and the greater reason why you are doing it. For example, "I'm going to increase my stamina so I can play in the park with my kids." It's affirming a positive fixed belief that you can do as well as attaching that statement to a greater reason, your children.

A – ACCOMPLISHMENTS

Limited beliefs can stop you from acknowledging the small wins and deeming them irrelevant in your journey. The negative impact this has ultimately stops the smaller wins from turning in the bigger wins. For example, if you drank three litres every day for a week but fail to recognise this progress because your limiting beliefs tell you, "Yes BUT you're still a loser because you ate three KitKat this week and had full fat coke." you are taking away from celebrating the achievements. Start becoming aware of these limiting beliefs occurring in your weekly non-critical evaluation.

One of the biggest limiting beliefs I come across daily is that women believe that to lose weight and look good they need to make *sacrifices* and the process will be *difficult*. These limiting beliefs are the reason why women give up and throw in the towel so early on their journey. But where does this belief come from? It usually comes from peers and generations of seeing people battle to lose weight. Because of the amount of weight loss solutions that have existed over the years everything from the Weetabix diet, fasting, shakes etc we are used to seeing women struggle to follow through with fast-fixes and faddy diets in order to get a result. However, if you actually think of those peers around you who are healthy and maintaining their weight, they are usually the women who quite simply eat healthy and exercise regularly. The women who inspire you are the women who don't do anything faddy at all they keep it simple and aim purely for lifestyle. Creating a lifestyle doesn't involve sacrifices or struggle because simply put you have no intention of stopping you see it as a continual process. If you stop seeing weight loss as an end goal and start seeing lifestyle as the process that will take you there you will remove many of the limiting beliefs that are holding you back.

Key learnings from this chapter

- Choose Lifestyle not weight loss
- Identify and replace your limiting beliefs
- Sacrifices are not needed

I OWN IT

ACCOUNTABILITY MEANS OWNING IT IF YOU DO AND OWNING IT IF YOU DON'T

*A*ccountability is all about separating the dreamers from the action takers. If you desire to make a change in your life, you need to take inspired action. You can sit thinking about the changes you want to make, and, in some respect, you can make these changes seem simple enough in your mind to get started. Then when you begin to put the plan into action you forget about all the detailed actions that can help you and focus on the larger actions. When you think about weight loss you think about going to the gym. When you think about losing body fat you relate that to eating less. Yes, are these statements the bigger they are but where do the smaller detailed changes come into play and how do you ensure that they will be actioned? The key is looking at these huge lifestyle changes and breaking them down into simple, easier steps. For example if you need to eat less, start with working out how many calories you eat now and look to remove white carbohydrates for example. Then keep making the smaller changes needed until you eventually reach the bigger goal of eating less.

ACCOUNTABILITY.

Accountability means to record your actions and monitor the behaviours attached to those actions constantly whether they are good, bad, or mediocre. You recognise that these all contribute to your journey and help progress you towards the end goal. When the end goal is broad and the time it will take you to reach it is more longer-term accountability is the only method that will take you from A to B and help you create a plan. It can also help you when looking at what smaller goals and habits you need to create in the interim as you progress there.

Most of my ladies have the same goal – be in love with the girl they see in the mirror. Be confident, happy, and healthy and show up in life as the best version of them-selves. They may initially meet me and say they want to lose two stone, but I already know the bigger end goal they have in mind. We all want to be comfortable and confident in our own skin and no number on the scale is attached to that. So, when the goal is qualitative and not quantitative it's even more important to look at the plan and stay accountable to it. The chances are to reach a qualitive goal you need a quantitative plan to get there and that's where I keep my plans simple and straight forward for my clients to follow. The plan itself remains simple but the complex day to day improvements which occur are much more complex. These changes can only be identified through remaining accountable and analysing the detail.

For example, if the end goal is to achieve 100/100 in an exam and you scored 60. You wouldn't just keep repeating the same exam hoping at some point you'll hit 100. You'll try, try and try again until eventually you give up and decide it's not for you. This is exactly what people do when they begin a weight loss attempt. They do the basics and get frustrated when it doesn't work and then give up. If you really wanted to score 100 on the exam you would have to look at the forty things you did wrong and look at how you could improve on each of the forty areas. In time you would improve each time you sit the exam and see progress. The progress would drive you to eventually getting 100/100. The point I'm making is that unless you see progress on your journey to creating a body you love you won't believe it's possible to eventually hit the milestone. Accountability helps you see the details and identify where you can improve.

Weight loss is a broad term end result that most women want to achieve. As I said before, the real changes they want in their life are even broader than that so how do we create a plan to be accountable too? We need to look at all the areas that need improvement hence how I decided to design the *Plan to Glam* You need to look at the mindset, your nutrition, your exercise and your overall vision and become accountable for all four elements. You simplify the elements to create a plan and then analyse the detail weekly or monthly and make improvements.

Take a look at exercise for example you want to see an improvement in your step count score month on month. Most women who start with me only average 3000 steps a day so you wouldn't be looking at them doing 10000 steps by the end of month one. However if I set them a goal of 4000 they'd be much more likely to achieve it. How would they stay accountable? They would log their step count every single day. This would then add a conscious element to the goal to keep them both engaged and attached to the meaning from a positive psychology perspective.

The Dedication part of the *Plan to glam* is detailed enough to be constantly analysed, improved upon and details added. The key is keeping it achievable and knowing that you will be constantly taking steps to improve. If I simply told you to go the gym twice a week for 45 minutes and each time you went you did the same thing it's highly unlikely you'd reach your goal. The lack of accountability and progression would eventually encourage you to give up. Many women approach me and tell me they've been training for years and never actually looked any different. There is a woman who comes to my mind who I see each time I attend my own local gym who does an hour on the treadmill every evening and she's done it for years but progressed nowhere. It all comes down to accountability and progression.

There are many ways to stay accountable and different ways work for different people.

SELF-MONITORING

The definition of accountability is taking personal responsibility of your actions, so the myth people have are needing to someone to hold them accountable is completely false. When you're personally accountable, you take ownership of situations that you're involved in. You see them through, and you take responsibility for what happens – good or bad. You don't blame others if things go wrong. Instead, you do your best to make things right. To stay accountable personally you need to look at what areas you need to improve on constantly and be open to making changes and learning different ways and techniques of doing things. For example, if you've been doing the same fifteen minute walk on the treadmill for six weeks, it's for you to look and see where you can improve and make it more challenging i.e. add in one minute jog every other minute. You'd do that for six weeks and then look to improve on it again.

LOGGING AND ANALYSING DATA

One of the greatest things about body transformation goals is that due to technology we have so much data automatically generated for us that we don't even have to try to log everything. We have smart watches which can analyse out heart rate, calorie burn, minutes spent training, our daily step count. And we have apps that will help us to monitor our food, count the calories for us and even tell us how much of each **MACRO** we are consuming. We can instantly see and monitor improvements using apps such as Fitbit, myfitnesspal and then use the data to help us improve and step it up a level.

EXTERNAL ACCOUNTABILITY

This is where I come in! Hiring someone to keep you accountable and help you continually improve can certainly help you on your journey and help you reach the goals quicker than you would on your own. I even have clients who left the studio over a year ago check in with me and share their progress. Equally you can get a friend or a gym buddy to train with, so you have someone to discuss your progress with weekly and look at improvements.

SOCIAL MEDIA

Recording progress pictures, weigh ins and food picture to help create a diary of progress works wonders when it comes to accountability. If you visually record everything you do, you'll be able to monitor your progress and keep the variety. Most people who create online diaries often follow other people doing the same thing as well as people who inspire them for recipes and workouts.

When becoming accountable for our actions we need to look at what is working as well as what's not. We often attach labels to ourselves and our actions which can have a negative impact on the goals we are working on. Labels have been applied to us from a young age. Those labels reflect how we feel about ourselves, how others perceive us and how we think when we go about our daily routines. When working on creating a healthier happier you there are many labels which need addressing and these are not just the labels you've given to yourself. They are the labels you've given your eating habits, your ability to be successful and the habits that you've already formed.

Jo, has always labelled herself as "fat". After just a week of training with her I noticed she often labelled herself nega-tively when carrying out her workout. *"I can't jump I'm too fat." "I can't lift that weight I'm weak." "I don't have any strength in me whatsoever."* I noticed the language she was using straight away was going to be harmful to her progress. I could tell Jo had no awareness of her negative self-talk and labelling so I decided to start keeping notes on my phone. After the second week of training, I showed her a list of fifteen things she's labelled herself as. She was shocked to see her own choice of words. Did she believe she's all those things? She didn't. She believed that by applying those labels she wouldn't be so disappointed when she gave up or hadn't made any progress when I weighed her.

Ask yourself are there any labels you may be applying to yourself that are harmful to you progressing with creating the body you love. Listen to not just the things you're vocalising but what you are saying yourself internally whilst you are carry out certain tasks. Negative self- talk will prevent you from remaining accountable.

I tasked Jo with replacing the fifteen negative self-talk statements with fifteen new statements to help form new habits and remain accountable. I've listed them below, feel free to steal her amazing ones or create your own .

I am getting stronger everyday
I'm so proud of my body
Working out is easy and fun
There's no restrictions on what I can do
I open to learning
I'm going all in on new experiences
I know I'm capable of anything
My weight doesn't hold me back

I am happier when I am healthy
I enjoy coming to the gym
I am healthy
I love who I am becoming
I am learning to exercise
I want to get better
I have nothing stopping me

I've always enjoyed reading and researching the impacts of good habits on our lifestyle. Habits make up 40% of our daily life, most daily tasks we complete are done without thought because they are part of our routine. That's why when looking at behaviour change, we often talk about forming new habits that will support the change or goal we are looking to achieve. In the world of weight loss, the impact of small habits can have huge impacts on achieving our goals. Habits create the foundations of our lives. Whatever you're in the habit of thinking, believing and doing determines the 'reality' you experience. Hence becoming aware of, and getting control over, your habits is one of the most important things you can do when it comes to changing your life.

Procrastinating is a habit, being on time is a habit, eating well is a habit, indecision is a habit, being negative is a habit, staying broke is a habit, being successful is a habit, having arguments is a habit – we carry out our behaviours on autopilot and often, unconsciously, accept them as 'the way things are.'

Zara, has been training with me now for six months. For the first three months of training with me she would never eat meals. She would constantly snack all day long, staying in her calorie count but her routine was all out. She would go to bed at 1am and I found it hard to manage her food diary because of her habits. She would drink nearly 600 kcals a day and the rest of her food was made up from snacks. As you can imagine Zara's results were nowhere near as good as they should have been. She was losing weight and toning up but at the same time the progress was being held up by her eating habits.

The good news is, when it comes to the habits that are making your life miserable and preventing your success, all you have to do is wake up to the fact that they are indeed merely habits, remember that you can change your habits, and then do what it takes to change them. Creating new, positive habits is what we need to do to create the body you love and live a healthy lifestyle.

Most of us realise that when we repeat something enough times, we establish new neural pathways in the brain that our habit flows through effortlessly and becomes automatic. Here are some elements involved in habit creation:

The Trigger – trigger sends signals to our brain that it's time to perform a habit. The trigger is usually something physical i.e. you're leaving for work, using the bathroom etc. The trigger however can be emotional when it comes to habits around food. I'll cover that more in Chapter 9.

The Sequence – habits work in a sequence that starts with a trigger and then leads to a response which then leads to a reward.

The Repetition – repetition requires mental and physical effort at first but over time, it becomes second nature. This is why at first running on the treadmill seems ridiculously hard but after a few months it becomes natural to walk up to the treadmill and begin your warmup.

The Ease – the easier things are, the more likely you're to do them. When creating new habits, the easier you make them the more likely they will stick. So, if you want to start taking multi vitamins for example put them next to your contraceptive pill so they work into your routine with ease.

The Patience – most habits take more time than you think, so stick with doing it consciously until it forms part of your routine. Drinking water whilst you're working at first seems like a chore but within weeks, you'll find yourself automatically drinking it during a meeting.

The Identity – habits are more than just the actions we take, habits are our beliefs, thoughts and words. This is why using the affirmations in this book are all designed at changing your belief system into creating a lifestyle and body you love.

Taking time to learn more about your triggers, routines and taking control of your habits is one of the most important jobs you can do. It gets you out of the victim mode and puts you in the driver's seat. Habitually setting healthy boundaries lays the groundwork for all other habits.

If you're getting into avoiding white bread for example, you may reconsider eating at an Italian restaurant, switching the bread you'd usually keep at home and informing those who you eat out with that there are certain foods you won't be touching. Your boundaries define the space you require to show up as the best version of you

Pay attention to three common types of boundary enemies:

Saying yes when we mean no - we say yes to everything in order to avoid confrontations, disappointing others or appearing selfish.

Too much no – we say no for fear of being seen, disappointed, or looking too fussy.

Becoming too controlling – we try to control other people, get them to take on our problems, become overly involved in their problems. Remember we are working on ourselves not changing the world.

When setting boundaries, we want to be nice, to bring joy to others, to be good, helpful, agreeable, compassionate, popular people. We think that compromising our boundaries is the best way to meet those needs. We fear that by setting a boundary, we're cutting off ourselves from others. Meanwhile, clearly defining who you are and what you're available for isn't selfish but rather it's remaining accountable and staying focused on the task in hand – looking amazing. The better you get at setting good, clear boundaries of your own and respecting those of others, the easier your life will become.

So how do we create new habits that will help us reach our goals?

1. Create new mantras – Using the affirmations in this book or creating new ones that eliminate the old habits we're trying to move away from. Write it down and say it out loud every day. The power is all in repetition and connecting with the feeling of excitement.
2. Come up with a list of small habit changes that will support your bigger goals. Make a list of at least fifteen things you'll do to set yourself up for success. Tiny steps you take consistently add up to big changes.
3. Remain accountable using all the tools we've already discussed in this chapter
4. Link your new habits to your existing habits to make them easier.
5. Ignore negative self-talk and avoid attaching labels to your actions.
6. Reward yourself.

7. Surround yourself with greatness, human and otherwise. Whether you realise it or not, you're enormously influenced by who and what surrounds you. Your environment can either make or break you faster than almost anything. Making smart choices about your environment is one of the best decisions you'll make in your life.

8. Remember to do them! You're here to flourish. By doing this, you're not only living a healthier life, you're inspiring others around you.

9. Talk about it constantly. Your words anchor your reality, whether you like it or not. If you talk about being fat, that's what people will see you for. If you talk about being lazy, that's what you eventually settle yourself into. Watch your words. And everyone else's.

10. Step into your confidence. Any fears, doubts, worries you have about yourself and your fabulousness were learned from the people around you and from your own temporary failures. They are far from the truth. The truth is you were born confident. It's not something you need to go out and buy. It's already who you are.

And lastly give thanks. Gratitude is something you get to choose consciously. You've experienced a temporary setback so you could learn from it. Be grateful for your mind, body and soul for the experience. Be grateful for the person you're becoming. Use this feeling of gratitude to stay motivated and take the next step.

Attaching accountability to positive psychology will help us flourish and progress faster on our journey to create a body we love, form the new habits we need to progress and eliminate those negative labels we've attached. I've summarised how positive psychology will really support when remaining accountable.

P - POSITIVE EMOTION

Connecting to your progress is the key to remaining positive as you analyse your success and results. Removing negative language from your vocabulary and replacing it with positive mantras will help you remain focuses and progressing week on week. Each week you need to be praising at least two things you've done that are contributing to your success i.e. taking the stairs at work, or avoiding the vending machine. It's these small things that make the progression count.

E – ENGAGEMENT

Accountability is exactly what keeps you engaged on your journey so decide which method of accountability you are using or even create a combination of the different methods shared above and use those to keep track.

R – RELATIONSHIPS

Choose the people who will keep you accountable wisely. If they're a professional, you want to look at exactly which data they'll be monitoring and feeding back on. For example, a personal trainer may not look at your nutrition and vice versa. Ensure their area of specialism is your area of weakness and choose a mentor who you inspire to be. Your mentor needs to be someone you look at and which to embody their qualities into your personality. They should be positive, supportive, and cheerleading you at all times.

M – MEANING

Keeping your eye on the bigger picture can be difficult when you're looking at small ways to improve. Remember to keep your visualisation alive daily and imagine the transformation as already being done. That way when you are looking at your improvements you already the exact reason why the effort is needed for the smaller changes.

A – ACCOMPLISHMENTS

Luckily on your quest for your dream body there's so much to celebrate. Make sure when you are looking at the detail you are highlighting what's going well. The key is making sure those little wins continue into the next week and don't get left behind so by acknowledging them you are ensuring they carry over into the rest of the weeks.

Key Learnings from this chapter

- Small improvements lead to big changes
- Make building habits part of your journey
- Remove the negative labels you've attached to yourself, food and others

I LOVE THE BODY I AM CREATING

IN EVERY WOMAN LIVES A QUEEN....

For me a queen is becoming the best version of yourself and being completely unapologetic for who you are. A queen is confident and holds her own at all times. She knows her strengths and uses them to achieve everything she desires. Weaknesses don't come into play and every problem will be handled and overcome. A queen takes responsibility for what she can control and holds no one else responsible for her life. She prioritises self-care and knows her struggles mean she's worth every second she invests into herself.

You hear my passion, right? I genuinely believe every woman deserves to feel like a queen. I say queen and not princess intentionally. A queen creates it all for herself without relying on anyone else. A princess is sat expecting everyone else to take care of her. My journey to becoming a queen wasn't an easy one but to create a body you love you need to step into your birth right of becoming a queen and avoid being sucked into the mundane routines that we as women are constantly pulled towards.

Sadly, I meet women every day who have become used to putting themselves last on the priority list. We're expected to be the doting wife, amazing mother, perfect housewife, working mum and take care of extended family, keep up the housework and quite frankly we run the show. And the result of us playing superwoman we neglect the very one thing that needs preserving, our health. I say health and not body for a reason. I don't believe the external elements of looking good and being the best version of ourselves result in us becoming a queen. It's the work we do internally on our mindset and externally it's the effort we put into creating the healthiest version you can be.

It's for this reason that queens come in all shapes and sizes because as long as being healthy is your goal the number on the scale is irrelevant. Whenever I meet women for the first time, they will happily talk for twenty minutes about the number on the scale they used to be, and how they used to look in their twenties. Some even come in with a photograph showing me that's when they last looked their best self. As we go through life the past versions of ourselves become irrelevant and what matters is the here and now. Chasing an image of yourself from the past will never come to fruition. The focus needs to be of becoming the best version of yourself right now. That's because your circumstances are different to what they were then, you've probably aged and the true reason you've come to me is because you want to *feel* the way you did in that photograph. Healthy, happy, and confident.

As your circumstances change and your responsibilities become greater the focus on yourself becomes less and less and before you know it you look in the mirror and are unrecognisable. We scroll through social media whether it be Snapchat, Instagram or Facebook and look at everyone else and what they are doing. Do they still look good for their age? How do they manage it? Have they got the same life stresses as you? You end up evaluating your own life and wondering how you can make a change that's going to help you get back to where you were. It's depressing and it pulls you down.

You may follow celebrities whose lives seem perfect. You see them have children and snap back into shape. Their bodies seem to be perfection and you can't help but look in the mirror and think what it is that's happening to me that I can't control. You may know but one of my biggest pet peeves on social media is the way advertising and marketing for all things weight loss is presented. You have ads from people being paid large amounts of money to show you the reason they are 'so slim' or have 'fast-acting weight loss' or are 'super toned' is because of some miracle machine or magic potion that's miraculously melted their fat and made them look amazing. It's a fact that it's impossible any faddy product has made a difference and they are in fact eating healthy and exercising. Did the product make a slight difference, possibly? I'll let you judge that. The thing is we know the majority of what we see on social media is edited or manipulated to make us do one thing - purchase and spend our hard-earned cash. How many weight loss ads have you leaned towards and either nearly purchased or already have?

Why? We already know you don't 100% believe what you are reading. It's because we are being sold the dream and the marketing is leading towards one thing – our low self-esteem. We believe the reason we are not living as the best version as ourselves is because our weight is stopping us, or that if we looked a little better on the outside, we'd ultimately be happier. This will never be the case. The work that needs to be done is internal and starts primarily with our mindset. To look good on the outside we need to invest on creating the queen mentality I talk about in this chapter. The queen who is deserving and works on herself daily.

Before and after pictures have never been my thing. I have carried out some amazing body transformations from people who've lost huge amounts of weight, to women toning up after giving birth, to women gaining muscle and creating curves. Transformations are amazing and I make a lIving doing it, but what I'll never do is lean towards the social media trend of selling the 'dream body' and telling you, you will achieve the same. Before and after pictures on social media are widespread. Do I believe they are real people? Yes, I do but are they replicated with different brands and faddy weight loss products yes. Do I believe they did nothing but just use that product? Absolutely not.

Working as a body transformation coach, there is one quality that all my ladies who have the dramatic before and afters have had in them: perseverance. They will always be ready to learn, try new things and seek improvement constantly. They believed in the end goal, they attached meaning and they constantly always showed up as their best self. They believed that they'd achieve it no matter what. They knew hard work would pay off. They knew they must remain dedicated to the plan. They knew the work they were putting in was for them alone and no one could do it for them. This belief system is not available to purchase via social media for $37.

This is the mentality of a queen.

A queen mindset aligns completely with the Mindfit mindset we talk about in this book supporting you in creating a body you love. Mindfit mindset consists of three elements – self-love, self-confidence, and self-belief. All qualities of the queen you are becoming.

In this chapter we are going to look at these three elements and how we can embody them and use them to empower us on the journey to creating the body you love. The first element is self-love and I wanted to share my own journey.

> *"She really loves herself."*

> *"Who does she think she is?"*

> *"She thinks she's so pretty!"*

These are all things that have been said behind my back, to my face and written on my social media posts in the past two years since opening my studio. Prior to opening the studio, I was a very private person but working on myself had happened years before. It wasn't always that way.

When I was 13,14, I became part of the crowd that grew up a little bit earlier than they should and every girl who I spent time with had a boyfriend. I was brought up well in a working class family but for some reason I wanted to be like the girls I hung around with in the evenings. I started to become self-conscious and begun to stare at myself in the mirror daily wanting to change the way I looked. I would stand in the mirror for hours wondering how I could get the older boys to like me. I didn't feel pretty. I felt miserable most of the time and to cover it up I started wearing makeup and trying to make myself feel pretty. I know some of you reading this can relate whether this happened to you at 13/14 or a later age we all have that moment where we don't quite know exactly who we are.

I'd excluded myself from my usual crowd of friends in school and kept leaning towards the type of girls who now as a mum wouldn't let my own children go anywhere near. I became dependant on their approval and all I wanted was to be more and more like them. Make-up, short skirts anything that would make me more 'attractive'. The girls would pick on me and laugh at my attempts to beautify myself. They'd push me towards older men and then laugh at me trying ridiculously hard to be liked. The girls I'd aspired to be were now bullying me.

I didn't feel like I knew who I was or who I wanted to be, so I confided in a teacher about the way I was feeling. It is the conversations I had with this amazing teacher, Mrs Ali, who helped me become the woman I am today. She didn't judge what had been going on with the other girls she took the time to invest in helping me uncover my character strengths, focus on who I wanted to be and helped me align my mindset to not caring about the approval I so desperately sought from the group of girls.

Needless to say, none of these girls ever amounted to anything. Not that I wish bad on anyone but if I hadn't begun to work on myself at the age of fifteen with Miss Ali, I don't want to imagine the path that I may have taken. I hold credit to that teacher and always have. My first daughter is even named after her.

Self-love is all about understanding who you are as a person and not living by other people's perception and opinions about you. Your value and self-worth is not defined by how you look on the outside and that's why chasing a number on the scale will never fulfil you. It's about being truly aligned to who you are on the inside and that simply projects on the outside.

To develop your appreciation for yourself, try these two positive psychology techniques that will develop your own self-appreciation and self-love and get you on track for creating the Mindfit mindset.

SELF-APPRECIATION

Think about the journey you've already come on, what barriers have you already overcome, how did you survive the difficulties and challenges and ultimately how has that has defined your character.

Write these out in a journal. Praising yourself on how you've handled experiences and lessons you have taken from them is all part of character building.

In order to love yourself you cannot hate the experiences that have shaped you, you must acknowledge the learnings you've taken from them and apply that to your character.

PERSONAL STRENGTHS

Strength finding is a huge element of positive psychology and I run detailed workshops on really discovering who you are as a person. If you've never done this before I highly recommend you spend some time looking into it.

The VIA strengths finder has a free test on their website www.viacharacter.org this test helps identify your five top strengths out of a list of 24. Once you understand your personality you can understand the reasoning of how you handle specific situations, and you are the way you are. The deeper connected you are to your character the more you and love and appreciate yourself.

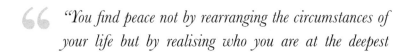 *"You find peace not by rearranging the circumstances of your life but by realising who you are at the deepest level"*

— *ECKHART TOLLE*

The second element of the Mindfit mindset is self-confidence. To become the best version of yourself, self-confidence is a key element. Self-confidence means trusting your own judgement, capacities, and abilities. We've just looked at your character strengths, so this is about how you use those to inspire you to take action and believe in your capacity to make anything happen. This is when I get excited when I see in women their true belief that they can in fact create a body they love and step into the shoes of a woman who truly loves the skin they live in. It's about valuing yourself and feeling worth regardless of any imperfections or anyone else's opinions.

Self-efficacy and self-esteem are often discussed alongside self-confidence. Self-efficacy is when we see ourselves mastering skills and achieving goals. This is what *Plan to Glam* aims to help you achieve by constantly recognising the wins you build your self-efficacy.

Self-esteem is more a general feeling that we have the right to be happy and accept circumstances as they come and don't allow them to phase us. Self-esteem means we can reject other people's opinions about ourselves and disregard the need for approval. It's your self-esteem that often causes you to not stay focused on your end goals. When it comes to creating the best version of you, you cannot allow others' opinions of you to define who you are and what you are trying to achieve.

One of the biggest issues affecting my client's self-confidence is comparing themselves to others. Comparison triggers an emotion in people that's difficult to control and in the world of weight loss can be so damaging to your journey. Imagine you've walked through the school yard, and you see Claire who used to go to school with. Claire used to be overweight at school and here she is on a glorious Monday morning walking through the school yard with her three children looking amazing. She's dressed well, looks good and you're walking towards her in your jog pants having just rushed the kids out of the door. How you'd react in this situation determines your self-confidence.

Would you

- Stare her up and down and wonder how on earth she looks that good. And then go home, phone your friend, stalk her Instagram and then talk about her for the next day or so.
- Walk up to her, compliment her, ask her how she lost all her weight and then start the same thing she's doing the following Monday.
- Stop and chat to her, apologise for how awful you look and spend the next ten minutes telling her how you've let yourself go and don't know what to do about it.

All of the above links to low self-esteem and low self-confidence. To build your confidence, you need to identify the triggers that cause you to act in a certain way. All the elements we've talked about in the book are going to help you do that – plus you have me as a cheerleader.

Making a solid plan into achieving your goals and believing wholeheartedly in your capabilities to it will build your self-confidence and allow you to flourish. If you want to see the true queen in you come out you need to be able to walk straight past the likes of Claire and not even flinch because you know where you are on your own journey and that you are already working on becoming the best version of you. That's the confidence I'm talking about!

The last element of the Mindfit mindset is self-belief and this my queen is believing that the journey you are on right now and the plan you have created to give you the ultimate success will take you from where you are now to where you need to be. I'm writing this book right now with true belief I have exactly what it takes to make it a best-seller and become an author. It's the belief in that any dream can be made into a reality and for me this is a lifestyle change for many.

Every January I sit and update my manifestation board. For those of you who don't know what that is it's basically a board where you place up your goals and visions for the future and focus on them daily to help you stay focused and goal driven. You don't have to be overly spiritual to believe in the power a manifestation board. Manifestation simply put is bringing your dreams into reality and believing whole-heartedly you can achieve them. Manifestation doesn't define the "how" it works by helping you focus on the result and visualising yourself achieving it. I've included visualisation in this book as it's one of the mindset tools I use often to help bring my dreams to reality.

I'll share with you my manifestation board for 2020. I find visuals that represent the goal I wish to bring to reality. The first thing was my business card for Glam Fit Studios my vision was to build a successful boutique gym. The second thing was £3000. The next was a picture of a picture of Dubai. These may seem very materialistic to you don't worry this is just my personal goals, yours may be completely different. I also chose a word of the year in which I wanted to embody daily. My word for 2020 was "Success" I clearly didn't know a pandemic was coming but ultimately what I wanted in 2020 was to build a successful business. I would stare at this board every morning to help me stay focused and I would visualise myself living that life as if it was already happening.

Here's how to make manifestation work in terms of body transformations. It's all about visualising the person you are becoming and creating goals around what the best version of you will be doing. Will you be ordering clothes from a certain shop, in which case your visual would be that store. Will be eating certain foods; in which case it could be a picture of a healthy smoothie. Will you be out enjoying your time with friends or going on a holiday with your kids etc. Whatever the goal attach a visual to it and focus on it daily. This will help develop the self-belief that you are in fact capable of achieving it and it's already happening for you.

LIVING YOUR BEST LIFE

So as a queen I want all the women around me to become a queen too. I want them to step out of their own shadow and into the footsteps of a woman who can do anything. In positive psychology we are constantly striving towards every area of our life being fulfilled. So, I wanted to share with you a life coaching tool I've been using for years to keep track of every area of my life to ensure I flourish in all aspects.

The circle of life tool is sometimes referred to as the wheel of life and helps put a measure on all areas of your life. If you are living your best life and are totally fulfilled every area of the circle will be full if not you will be able to see the areas of improvement. You give yourself a rating of 1-10 on each aspect of the circle and then create your goals to help work towards filling your circle. I've included my own downloadable version of the circle on www. mindfitmindset.com

If focusing on you is now going to be part of the new version of you then you will love using this tool. Ultimately you deserve to be looked after, you deserve to show up as your best self and you deserve the body of your dreams. By evaluating every area of your life, you identify the areas you need to work on to improve.

One of my clients, Ishrat was about to reach her weight loss goal and was coming to the end of the body transformation package she'd been completing with me. She came to me in the last week and was so excited about the changes she had made to her lifestyle. She'd chosen a gym she was going to join, she was happy with her food choices and was well on her way to ensuring her health was always going to be a priority. It's in these moments I know I've done my job correctly because I see the passion and enthusiasm they must keep going. She had one concern. What would be her goal now if she had finished working with me and all the goals had been achieved.

I introduced her to the life cycle activity, and she was blown away. The sections on the life circle vary from circle to circle but ultimately include your home life, your friends and family, your spirituality, your career/income, your health, your fun, your personal development. The list can be different for each wheel. So, I asked Ishrat to complete the wheel of life. The health section was naturally at a ten because she was confident, she knew where she was going. She identified a gap in her spirituality, she hadn't been praying as regular as she used to. So I helped her set some new goals around achieving a ten on the circle of life and that became her new focus for the next three months.

What I'm trying to get you to understand is that there's always elements of your life that need improving. It's rare you are fulfilled in all aspects unless you actively monitor it constantly and seek improvement. A queen knows nothing will come to her with ease she will need to go out and get it. There's self-development to be done constantly and goals need to be continually updated and set. To always show up as your best self you need to continually be working on yourself.

Key Learnings from this chapter

- Queens work on themselves continually
- Self-love is an appreciation for your strengths
- Confidence comes when you ignore others and work on you

I AM DEDICATED

DREAMS AND DEDICATION ARE A POWERFUL COMBINATION

*Y*ou wake up in the morning look into the mirror and imagine you look like the woman we created in Chapter 4, you put on your gym gear, prep your meals for the day and are about to step out of the door when your phones rings.... It's school and your little one needs collecting urgently with a bout of DV. Your plans are thrown out for the day whilst you quickly rush to collect them and make sure they're comforted and on the mend.

Having your day interrupted by emergencies and unexpected events often throw you off. As a mum of five it happens to me regularly. Everything from the washing machine leaking, kids forgetting their pack lunch, urgent doctors' appointment, parents needing me, overtime required for work, food needing preparing... the list goes on and on. As women we have responsibilities that stretch way beyond the simple routine of getting up, working, going to the gym and then having an early night that's why remaining dedicated to the plan that we have created is key to success.

It's for that reason I like to keep the 'Dedication' part of the plan simple and realistic. There may be weeks where you can go above and beyond two gym sessions and one walk and that's amazing but it must be seen as a bonus and not a must. To remain dedicated, you need to be able to reach your goal weekly regardless of the surrounding circumstances. Will there be weeks where you are so ill in bed it's impossible? Of course, but the key is remaining dedicated to rescheduling and rearranging.

When women contact me to sign up for weight loss programmes one of the first questions, I ask is what is driving them to get started today. Some women are all in and are ready to get started the following day or the following Monday and I can often hear the urgency in their tone of voice or by the fast pace typing in the DM. Most businesses wouldn't hesitate in taking their bank details and signing them up, but for me it's important to understand where they are in their journey. When you look at the faddy weight loss options out there they usually involve a hefty first purchase of a fast-action weight loss miracle shakes. Most faddy options require a first purchase between £100 - £300, and that's because they know the customer will most likely only ever make one purchase with them, two if they are lucky. You'll even notice the checkout pages on these websites pop up very easily because the quicker they take your money the better. But why is this?

This is not just the psychology of buying, it's the mindset that you're in when you are shopping around for a solution to your problem. When signing someone up to my programmes I look at "Is this person determined or dedicated?" The difference between the two tells me if this person will carry out the 90-day plan and really wants the lifestyle change and not the quick fix.

Determination is the powerful emotion that's provoked when we want to make change. It's a highly charged emotion which is usually driven from a place of frustration, despair, or negative experience. Quite possibly the reason you purchased or started to read this book. In the industry of weight loss this powerful emotion often leads you to sign up to things without thinking. Something we're all guilty of and you can most likely relate. If you are in this mindset right now don't worry this book is exactly what you need to start understanding the part your emotions and mindset play in terms of getting you results. It's more important to be aware of it and recognise these emotions to help support you on your journey.

One of my clients, Sara was signed up to four different app subscriptions on her phone with no real knowledge of what any of them could do for her. When I asked her about them, she could barely describe what each one did but what she did know is that when she signed up to them she was is a place of determination and a place of wanting immediate change. It's for this reason she was happy to hand over the cash but rarely even looked at the app after 24hours of purchasing. Did she need the app? Most likely not but the mindset she was in at the time told her she needed to purchase it immediately. She was in a place of determination.

Dedication, however is the longer-term solution to getting results and achieving your goals. It's the difference between the guy in the office who always succeeds and the one who starts amazing projects and never finishes them. In terms of weight loss, it's Laura on the front cover of the slimming magazine who's reached her goal weight in just 18months, looking incredible and glowing. But if you are more like my client Sara above you will now have signed up to another few faddy programmes staring at this magazine wondering how it happened for Laura and not you.

Dedication is all about connecting your motivations, the reasons you started, to a plan. That plan starts off with the understanding there is no short-term fix and that we are aiming for results. The is the "A" for accomplishment in the positive psychology PERMA model we discussed in Chapter 4. If you create a plan that's rewarding and sustainable then accomplishment is highly likely. Compare this to a purchase made whilst in a place of determination and you can start to understand the reasons why your weight loss attempts in the past may have failed or been short lived.

Keeping it simple.

Dedication is about the long-term vision and the journey of how you plan to get there.

Determination is looking for a short-term solution and getting a quick fix and this is exactly why I take the time out to discuss with every client their personal reasons for starting, their motivations, and their understanding of how they plan to get there. I want to know how dedicated they are.

So how do you remain dedicated? The answer lies in the positive psychology PERMA model and ensuring your plan includes all of the elements. Feel free to look at the below and then revisit your plan to make any tweaks.

P – POSITIVE EMOTION

Making sure your plan is enjoyable is key to its success. Firstly, look at the plan, are the activities you've planned something you enjoy doing? Would training with a friend, a group or alone work best for you? Exercise releases endorphins to give you that natural high so making sure your activity is one you enjoy is key to maximising that. You may find certain physical activity boring or stale. In that case change it up and instead choose something you enjoy or recruit a trainer to help you learn new ways to exercise effectively.

Secondly acknowledge your improvements on a weekly basis using my non-critical evaluation technique. This literally takes minutes and is game changing in the world of self-improvement and remaining dedicated. It's called non-critical because you simply evaluate yourself with the vision of improving step-by step. This way there are no disasters or 'falling off the wagon' because you're always focused on improvement. This evaluation is all about short term improvement.

WEEKLY NON-CRITICAL EVALUATION

Draw up three columns in the note section in your diary or your journal.

Your three columns are Stop, Start and Continue and you will write two *bullet points in each that are realistic for the next* seven *days.*

The STOP column is two *things you won't be doing for the next seven days, acknowledging what didn't go well.*

The START column is two *new things or changes you will make immediately. Be careful not to make these too elaborate.*

The CONTINUE column is all about praising the things that did go well.

All of your points should be specific and helping you reach your larger long-term goal.

Here's an example:

STOP

Skipping lunch and rushing to prepare my tea.

Having a coke can to give me energy.

START

Bringing my water bottle to work.

Find two healthy snacks I like.

CONTINUE

Going to gym straight after work without coming home

Not eating from the work canteen

Doing the non-critical evaluation keeps it basic and achievable. It doesn't involve you over stretching yourself and helps fuel the positive emotions needed to achieve the "P" in the Perma Model

E – ENGAGEMENT

Staying engaged with the plan we've created is the key to long-term success. You've taken the time out to write it, understand the theory behind it, program your mindset so now you need to look at staying engaged and excited by it.

The non-critical evaluation will certainly help you remain focused but to be engaged you need to be having fun doing it.

Remaining accountable by following your diary is a great way to do this. If you are logging your food, water intake and exercise in the diary it helps it become prominent in your daily routine. Using apps such as my fitness pal or Fitbit also have great visuals of your progress. There are so many measures of your new healthy lifestyle that you can engage with, and you can change these as you go through your plan, it doesn't always have to be the same visual that keeps you motivated and on track. I've listed a few below that my clients use to stay engaged and connected.

Step Count – Personally one of my favourites, seeing it gradually improve overtime as well as a boost when you've completed a long walk. Achieving your personal best is always a real buzz. I love when a client sends me their step count because they're proud of their personal achievement. It shows they are acknowledging all their wins and are really connected to their success.

Heart Rate – Watching your heartrate as you work out to see if you're at your optimal or even peaked at your highest after your hardest workout yet keeps you connected to your goals during the workout itself. Another element of your heart rate is to look at your resting heart rate. Over six to twelve months you will notice your resting heart rate has gradually decreased this is a clear indicator of your overall health improving.

Calories Burnt – If your smart watch logs your workouts for you, it's a great way to see how effective a workout is and which kind of workouts burn the most calories. Smart watches can also tell you your daily calorie expenditure from your step count and activity. Seeing that number increase as you get fitter and more active helps affirm that you are on track with your goals and that weight loss is a certainty.

Social Media Log – The modern scrapbooking method of recording your journey. Many of my own clients enjoy taking pictures of their food and exercise and uploading them to an online diary. It keeps them motivated and focused on their goals.

Photos – Many of my ladies take monthly progress photos of them in the same underwear or gym kit so they can visually see improvement and gain excitement over clothes becoming too big for them or seeing their bodies take on a new shape.

These are just a few ideas to help you stay engaged and connected to your journey. Avoiding falling into a stale boring routine which provides no enjoyment or buzz is the sure-fire way to lose your dedication so always find at least one way to stay connected to your journey.

R – RELATIONSHIPS

For many the journey of weight loss is very personal. Our goals are very different, our views vary and someone's opinion is not always what we need to hear. Many people express strong views on what you should and shouldn't be doing so who is your inner circle is extremely important. I've always the loved the Jim Rohn quote:

"You are the average of the five people you spend the most time with."

When it comes to creating a healthier, happier you, your circle of influence needs to be tight and supportive. One of my clients, Sairah, has always struggled with this. In her family she plays the lead role of hosting family events and cooking large quantities of food is a weekly task for her. The majority of the food would be by request of the family members and would be majority unhealthy. Once the food was cooked and served Sairah would be exhausted and eat not just the food cooked there and then but the leftover food for days afterwards. Her family members didn't support her weight loss and encouraged this routine regardless of how many times she'd told them she was trying to lose weight. When she attended events even if she had not cooked, she would be told that eating a chapati or two wouldn't harm her in anyway and therefore she was always under pressure to eat. Behind her back however they'd be sat discussing her unhealthy lifestyle offering critical advice whenever she brought up the issue.

Sairah's issue is probably one of the most common issues my ladies in the gym encounter and usually its driven by the ones closest to them so how do you create a new circle of influence and what kind of people could you include? I've created an example list below and I want you to write down in your journals who your five supportive people will be on your journey.

A friend or colleague who has already achieved their body goals.

Instagram account diary of someone with a similar lifestyle to you.

A personal trainer.

An accountability coach.

A friend or family member also on their journey to a healthier lifestyle.

A new friend you've met at the gym or in a class.

If you can't come up with five right now, don't worry keep a look out for who you might add to your circle of influence as you progress. Some of my greatest inspirations I've met whilst on my own journey were people who twelve-months ago I'd never come across so don't be afraid to find new people and engage in new relationships.

M - MEANING

To remain dedicated there must be meaning attached to what you are doing, and this means looking at how what are you are doing is for the greater good. In our case the greater good is flourishing in our health and wellbeing. For me this brings so much reward to every effort you put in, by understand the meaning to a healthier lifestyle you can begin to partake it activities you'd never dreamed of doing.

As part of your longer-term goals many women dream of an adventure holiday with their children, climbing a mountain or taking part in a charity run. These dreams always seem super ambitious when you first start out and it's easy to be in the mindset of, 'yeah right!' but having these longer-term goals established now and seeing them become a reality in twelve months time actually really helps drive your motivation and stay dedicated to the plan.

Jane was desperate to take her children on holiday, her inactive lifestyle had meant the children had spent most of the school holidays with other family members visiting the beach, days out at theme parks and having fun without her. She felt the reason for this was that she was too over-weight to partake or that she wouldn't be able to keep up. Therefore, it had become a habit that she just wouldn't come along. When she first came to me her reason 'why' was because she wanted to be the one to have fun with her children. When I asked her what that meant to her, she teared up and admitted it had been torturing her for years. When creating her *Plan to Glam* we attached this meaning to her plan and after six months of working with me I asked her to choose a date in which she'd go ahead with the weekend holiday. She was shocked, she replied "No I've only lost two stone I'm not there yet." I reminded her this was the reason we were doing this and got her to schedule a weekend away in three months' time, exactly what she'd been imagining. Needless to say the next three months she lost another 1.5stone purely driven by the fact we had scheduled the holiday. The holiday was everything she had dreamed it to be.

We attached the meaning to Jane's journey right from the outset, but we didn't actually schedule the goal until later in the journey and this could be the same for you. If your goal is to partake in a 10k run, you could schedule this in after three months into your journey. If your goal is to climb a mountain maybe schedule this after six months. This way you acknowledge the journey is not attached to a number on the scale or what dress size you are, it's purely around the meaning you attach to having a healthier lifestyle.

A – ACCOMPLISHMENT

Nothing helps you remain more dedicated than accomplishment. Celebrating your wins as you progress through your journey is one of the most important things to do. If you've got to this point in the book you will know by now the wins of weight loss stretch way further than the number on the scale. In fact, by now you should be so uninterested by the number you can already create a list of things to celebrate and I want you to be doing this constantly. Celebrate every win no matter how big or small.

Celebrate...

- The numbers – okay I'll let you have it.... Pounds lost, fat percentage drops, lowered BMI all count.
- An improvement in fitness – the first time you complete a walk, climb a hill manage a ten minute jog with ease.
- Attending an event and not being phased by the dessert table.
- Cooking a delicious healthy meal.
- Joining a new class you previously avoided.
- A friend or family complimenting your weight loss.
- Looking in the mirror fitting into that dress.

The list is endless, but you get the idea, every win is a win and log those wins weekly either in your noncritical evaluation or sharing with a friend.

Dedication is looking at all these different elements of the PERMA model so that your motivations and dreams become the reality. If you need to revisit your plan and add in any extras.

At this point in the book, I'd like you now consider losing the attachment you have to reaching a certain number on the scale. The more we talk about our visualisation and celebrating the vast amount of wins we can achieve on a weekly basis the less the numbers begin to matter. I totally get it when you begin your weight loss journey you automatically veer towards "needing to lose 2 stone" or " three stones lighter would make me happy" but I want you to begin looking at the bigger picture and the journey we are now embarking on to create the body you love. The body you love does not need a number and I'll talk about this more in Chapter 7.

You may believe that seeing a number reduce on the scale will be enough motivation to help you remain dedicated. In fact I ask my women to do the total opposite and stay away from the scales. I encourage all of the women I meet whether in person or online to only weigh themselves every four weeks. I get them to use the non-critical evaluation method as the measure of their success and we discuss this in our weekly chats. From over ten year's experience in helping women lose weight, I notice when you take away the focus on the scale women are more successful. If for example you've eaten really well all week but then when you jump on the scale and you've only lost 1lb it's sometimes disheartening and takes away from your successful week.

One of my clients Lynda used to be an avid member of weight watchers and would attend the weekly meetings without fail despite me advising her it wasn't needed. Each week she'd share stories from around the circle about how Tracey had eaten ice-cream that week and had still lost 3lbs or that poor Carla had eaten perfectly clean and had gained 1lb. Each week she'd come with the exact same stories until after eight weeks of me hearing the same thing repeatedly I asked Lynda, "Are you inspired by these other ladies?" It was rhetorical. I already knew the answer. The next two weeks she didn't go and she lost 5lbs on her next weigh in. She was so much happier without the pressure of the weekly weigh in and actually ended up losing more than she'd ever lost before purely because we'd taken away the emphasis on the number and improved her circle of influence.

Key Learnings from this Chapter

- Dedication is the long-term plan to achieve your dreams.
- Evaluate yourself weekly and get better in small steps.
- You are the five people you surround yourself with.

FOOD IS FUEL

CHOOSE PREMIUM

$\mathcal{Y}$ou can't expect to fuel up a diesel car with petrol and expect it to run.

You wouldn't starve your car of fuel and expect it start.

You wouldn't put £5 worth of petrol in and expect your car to drive from Preston to London.

This car analogy literally changed my life.

I'm always honest and open about the fact that I'm not a dietician nor do I claim to be. I hold several qualifications in nutrition and understand exactly what our body needs to function, burn fat and build muscle. If you are someone who has yo-yo dieted most of their life you could probably write this chapter yourself, but this chapter is focused on the mindset of eating not telling you or dictating to you what you should and shouldn't eat.

When I started to follow the concept of 'food is fuel' I was around the age of 24, prior to that I would binge on food, throw up or starve myself for weeks whilst carrying out a gruelling gym regime.

'Food is Fuel' is all about considering whether the food you are consuming is going to provide you with the right fuel you need to get through your day and I make every single food choice based on this theory. First of all you need to understand what fuel does body needs to function.

Energy – You need to consume enough food so that you are full of energy and able to go about your daily routine with ease. You need to power your workouts and still be able to look after the kids, cook food and hold down a job. If you are constantly burning out, the chance, are you are not providing yourself with enough kcals to power your lifestyle. What everybody needs is different and if you are ensure speak to a professional if you're struggling to get the right balance.

Nutrition – Getting the right balance of carbohydrates, fats and proteins are key to getting your fuel to work effectively for you. There are many apps such as Myfitnesspal that will do this hard work for you and tell you exactly what you are consuming on a daily basis. Once you have an understanding of your current consumption you can make the changes needed to help fuel your new lifestyle.

Vitamins and Minerals – Trying to obtain these through a healthy lifestyle requires a varied diet and therefore some people choose to take supplements but being deficient in any of these minerals will be directly impacting your health and energy levels.

Digestion – Ensuring you consume food that supports your digestive system and improves your metabolism.

Brain Power – supporting your cognitive function allows you to be as efficient as possible and avoids you getting sluggish and lethargic.

Body to heal/recover – Fuelling your body to recover whether it be from illness, exercise or injury is essential

The food your body requires consists of the above six fuels. Anything additional is not contributing to your overall health and wellbeing. 'Food is Fuel' means considering each time you eat the contribution that food is bringing to your health. If you only ate for fuel what would you consume?

At aged 24 I'd given birth to my first born I found that my energy levels had completely depleted. I was completely run down and exhausted constantly. At first I put it down to having the baby and it all being new to me. My diet consisted of mainly fast-food because I wasn't free to do the cooking. I relied on high sugar caffeine drinks, and sugar to spike my energy levels when I was feeling lethargic. I'd already arranged to return to work at twelve weeks because my high pressured job meant I needed to return as soon as possible. But I knew I wasn't right and I there was no way I could work on top of everything else. I'd gained five stones whilst pregnant and was left with an extra 2.5 stones to lose. But it wasn't the weight that bothered me, it was the fact I couldn't get up off the sofa. My energy had gone.

When Zayn was eight weeks old, he developed Bronchitis and was hospitalised for two weeks. I used to stay at the hospital 24hrs and was really struggling with my energy levels and asked the nurse for advice. She'd noticed my reliance on Red Bull and sugary snacks for energy already, so we began to chat. I'd told her how I was feeling, and I was worried it would lead to post-partum depression.

It turned out we both went to the same gym and although we'd never seen each other there we had a lot in common. She had just taken a qualification in nutrition and all the advice and tips she was sharing made total sense. I'd took on just a few small changes she'd recommended and within a few days I began to see an improvement entirely based on what I was eating. It was during my maternity leave I completed my first qualification in nutrition and the whole premise of the course was 'Food is Fuel'. I can honestly say if I didn't make those changes to my lifestyle ten years ago I would never be sat here writing a book about to create a healthy happier version of you. It's one of the reasons I love sharing my story with so many women.

Needless to say 'Food is Fuel' changed my whole outlook on how to eat correctly for my body. I ended up having all my children one after the other and within four and a half years I had five healthy children so it's a good job I did!

Whether your lifestyle involves working long hours, looking after children or being responsible for your house it *all* requires energy aka fuel to help get you through the day.

Working on your mindset of eating is one of the most powerful ways to change your eating habits. To do this we need to move towards mindful eating practices and understanding how our emotions are connected to the food we consume. There are two different types of hunger - emotional and physical. If you are an emotional eater, you may be already aware.

Emotional Hunger

- Emotional hunger comes on suddenly.
- Emotional hungers feels like it needs to be satisfied instantly.
- Emotional hunger craves specific comfort foods.
- Emotional hunger is not satisfied even on a full stomach.

- Emotional hunger triggers feelings of guilt, shame and powerlessness.

Physical Hunger

- Physical hunger comes on gradually.
- Physical hunger can wait.
- Physical hunger is open to options – lots of things sound good.
- Physical hunger stops when you are full.
- Eating to satisfy hunger doesn't make you feel bad about yourself.

If emotional eating is a struggle for you the key is identifying the routine and when and what times of the day it occurs. I always encourage keeping an eating diary whether it's digital or physical and update it in real time. When you update it at the exact time you are eating it will help you identify what caused you to eat i.e., was it physical hunger or emotional.

When Becky started logging her food, she felt the first two weeks was a disaster. She was completely honest and shared all the food she had eaten regardless of whether they were good or bad. She brought her diary along to the session and was down and depressed. Becky felt like she was failing. I opened the diary with a completely different approach, and I could see instantly there were two points of the day she was going off track, 2pm and 8pm. I asked her what specifically happened every day at 2pm. She told me she finished work and had to quickly rush home to get changed and ready for the school run. It was always a mad rush and because she doesn't get a lunch break, she's always hungry. I asked her what happened at 8pm every day and she again described her routine. The kids go to bed and I get "my time" so I sit on the sofa and watch old episodes of Friends. It's this information about her routine that I needed to know.

The key to overcoming emotional eating is to look at the pattern, the timing and the emotions surrounding that time of day. At 2pm Becky is exhausted, physically hungry but rushing. The emotional trigger of feeling like she has no time was causing her to emotionally eat high sugar foods. So, we looked at how we could interrupt her routine to avoid that happening. Becky suggested having a cup of soup around 1pm before her shift ended to satisfy her physical hunger. Within a week of introducing the new routine we replaced a can of coke and a kit kat with a cup of soup saving calories but also fuelling her body from physical hunger.

At 8pm Becky's routine of putting the kids to bed was stressful for her as she didn't feel like she had much alone time and therefore used to get angry and worked up getting the kids to be quiet. By the time she'd sat down to watch TV she felt she needed and deserved the crisps and hot chocolate even though she'd only eaten her healthy main meal an hour and a half before. Again, we looked at interrupting the routine. I asked Becky her suggestions as this needed to come from her. She decided to take the kids up fifteen minutes earlier and instead of coming downstairs straight away she would take a bath and get changed for bed before watching TV. This meant by 8.30pm she would sit and enjoy her episode of Friends without any need for the unnecessary food.

Interrupting your routine will allow you to be in control of your emotions. I was happy Becky had honestly logged her food because it was there in front of us in black and white exactly what the problem was. The key to emotional eating is understanding the reasons behind it and improving week on week. Nothing about Becky's first two weeks of eating were a failure they were educating us on what needed improving.

Mindful eating is all about considering the foods you're eating, being accountable and then consuming them consciously. People who mindfully eat their food usually consume 30% less food than someone who doesn't. Therefore, this is a habit you can't afford not to introduce to your daily routine. When the world was amazed by Adele's weight loss everyone was intrigued to know the techniques, she'd introduced to make such drastic changes. One of those shared by her nutritionist was Mindful Eating.

PLAN YOUR MEALS

Ideally you want to plan your weeks meals at the beginning of each week and it's most important to have planned your lunch and dinner. Based on the theory of 'food is fuel' create a meal that will fuel you for your busy day, workout or activity planned. Keep the week varied in terms of providing foods for nutrition and digestion. It may help to try and eat meals at the same times each day to fit your routine and consider the times when you experience physical hunger.

In order to plan your meals you must also keep the produce in your house ready for the meals you've planned. The only reason any of my ladies go off track is because either the food wasn't available and they needed to go shopping OR it would be time consuming to prepare the meal they'd chosen. The key is making it easy for you. If you know on certain days you are more tired than others then these are the days you keep it simple or you already have the food prepped in advance.

EAT WHEN YOU HAVE TIME

Okay so I can totally relate to there being no time in my schedule to eat. Anyone who is a busy mum, or working full time or both will struggle with rushing to eat and even worse eating whilst multi-tasking. So this will be a struggle for some of you but honestly a technique I never fault from. You need to eat when you have a good fifteen minutes to really enjoy consuming it so choose your time wisely. For some eating with the kids works, if you're like me with young children who need your attention constantly you may need to wait. One of my clients used to eat her evening meal at 7pm once the kids were in bed, so she felt full and didn't feel rushed.

Being consciously aware you are eating tells your brain that your body has been fuelled and is full. So, ensuring you take the time to enjoy every bite is important. Observe the food on your plate, appreciate the fuel you are providing your body and take your time to savour the food. You will also notice much more clearerly when you are full.

20-MINUTE RULE

Your body only recognises it is full twenty minutes after your last bite, so before you decide you need a dessert or something additional, allow your body the time it needs to acknowledge that you are full. This is the exact reason why when you eat when you are rushing you will never feel fulfilled.

LOG ALL YOUR FOOD

The more accountable you are the easier it is to improve on. And that's what you should be aiming for, improvement in your eating week on week. Log the food and drink you consume including the times you consume them. By logging it you understand it. Don't worry about what it looks like this is for you to improve on so worrying that it looks too much or it's not as "clean" as you'd like it to be is not beneficial here what we need to look at is the patterns.

After just the first week you can look at the following patterns in your eating.

- Look at the choice of foods – were they healthy?
- Did you have a variety or was it repeated?
- Did you feel full?
- What were your energy levels like?
- At what times were you hungry?
- Are you consuming enough fluids?

Using the non-critical evaluation method, you should only be giving yourself two improvements to make the following week, even if you need to change EVERY-THING. Aim for progress not perfection especially if healthy eating doesn't come naturally to you. I was there. I understand you.

STOCK UP ON HEALTHY SNACKS

Literally THE best tip I can give you especially for the emotional eaters is to have a cupboard in your house full of healthy snacks that you can easily consume. Most people choose to empty their cupboards when they begin a quest of healthy eating, but I tell them to do quite the opposite. Fill a cupboard in your house with at least ten snacks under 150kcals. This way whenever you feel an urge to snack you have plenty of options to fulfil that need and avoid the dart to the corner shop.

Creating your perfect food plan takes time to develop. Many industry experts and I, avoid creating plans for other people to follow because one plan can never fit the lifestyle of every individual. Your career, routines, allergies, taste buds etc all need to be taking into consideration. Always be on the lookout for inspiration whether be online, on social media or sharing recipes with friends. The key is keeping it focused on fuelling your body and supporting your goals. If in doubt seek professional advice from a dietician or nutritionist.

Positive Psychology and Mindful Eating go hand in hand when creating the body you love.

P – POSITIVE EMOTIONS

Developing a positive relationship with food starts with the acceptance that what you eat now can be improved even if it's just from the way you prepare and consume the food. To create a positive emotion around food it's important not to see what you are consuming as being deprived. If you feel your food is a punishment or you are simply doing it as a means to lose weight you are highly likely to revert back to your old diet the second your hormones kick in every month.

Layla, has an asian diet and most evenings consist of curry served with chapatis or rice. Her biggest concern is that to lose weight she will be forced to eat bland food every evening and not enjoy the food her mums has cooked. I remember her saying to me "There's no such thing as a healthy curry." It was clear to me her ability to follow a healthier eating plan had nothing to do with the food itself it was all about her mindset and the inability to see the options available to her. I instantly set her a task to prepare me a healthy curry and bring it in for me to try. Two days later she brought in the curry. The changes were simple. She changed the oil she had cooked it in, reduced the salt, added in some veg and instead of eating it with a chapati she had chosen a whole meal wrap. Her face was lit up and she couldn't wait for me to try it. I had no doubt it would taste amazing. So you see here the changes were in her attitude towards creating healthy options that she could enjoy and removing the negative opinions she had towards healthy foods.

E – ENGAGEMENT

To eat healthy, you must be acknowledging what you are eating and get into the habit of always having it at the forefront of your mind. After a year of conscious eating this may not be required but one of the biggest mistakes I see women make daily is when they attend their session with me, and they haven't completed their food diary. Your food diary needs to be completed in real time and you need to engage in improving it.

One of the best ways to stay engaged with your food is to take a picture of your meal before you consume it. All of my full-time body transformation clients must send me a picturew of every meal. They assume I want to see it so I can evaluate it or see if it's healthy but the majority of the time I don't offer commentary. I ask them to take the picture for their awareness of their food and so they remain accountable to the journey they've committed to. If you don't have a specialist, you could upload your pictures onto social media or send them to a friend or family member. This is all about accountability.

R – RELATIONSHIPS

Usually, your eating habits are affected by the people you surround yourself with. If those around, you are not consuming the same meals you are this can prove difficult. I always say where you can eat as a family, and you don't have distractions eat at the same time as them. I eat the same foods as my children I just may change it slightly. For example, I have brown pasta instead of white. It's important when mindfully eating that you don't exclude yourself even if your food is different, you must still integrate into your normal routine, anything too different and you run the risk of making your meal feel like a punishment.

M – MEANING

Attaching the reason why you are eating healthy to every meal you consume is so important. What you need to consider is whether your reason why is really your reason why. When I wanted to lose 2.5 of baby weight, and I did so five times over, my reason for eating healthy was not to lose weight. It wasn't about the 2.5 stone. The meaning we attach to our food needs to be the greater cause. The greater cause being a healthier happier you, having the energy to partake in a 10k run or being able to run around the park with your kids. The greater cause should inspire you to continue and the meaning you attach to each mouthful of food needs to be attached to this.

A – ACCOMPLISHMENT

Te success you achieve from eating healthy goes way beyond the scales and it will always be a case of progress not perfection. Even after ten years of healthy eating I am far from perfect and I'm always learning to introduce new foods and recipes. Celebrate as you improve and be inspired by others. You could aim for a new recipe each month or share your own ideas with others.

Key Learnings from this chapter

- Food is Fuel.
- Remain Accountable.
- Improve week on week – Progress not perfection.

WEIGHT LOSS IS CERTAIN

ACT AS IF IT HAS ALREADY HAPPENED

*E*ach chapter in this book starts with an affirmation to help you in creating the body you look. Positive affirmations are simply put a belief statement to help support a goal. On their own they don't create magic but are scientifically proven to have an impact on your subconscious beliefs. Every single day we are constantly putting out affirmations whether we say them aloud or in our head. The affirmations we naturally put out can steer us towards negativity and build reluctancy to change. For example, we look at the weather and affirm, "It's a miserable day.". We look in the mirror and say, "I look a mess." We open the fridge and say, "There's no food in the house." We have already affirmed several statements before we have even left the house in the morning so it's important to understand how these affirmations in our conscious mind connect to our subconscious mind to become reality.

The subconscious is the part of our minds that makes decisions without our needing to actively think about them. It's different from the conscious mind, which encompasses the thoughts we know we are having at any given moment. It's also different from the *unconscious* mind, which holds past events and experiences that we don't remember at all.

Our subconscious mind takes everything we say as fact, and these become our fixed beliefs. And as discussed in Chapter 5 we need to remove these limiting beliefs to allow change and success to happen. To bring around change we need to convince our subconscious mind that these things are already happening or have happened. This is the reason positive affirmations are commonly used and scientifically proven to drive success.

This book is created using ten positive affirmations to drive you on your journey to creating a body you love.

1. Mindset is everything.
2. I am worthy of a body I love.
3. I am capable of difficult things.
4. I have time to invest in me.
5. Anything is possible.
6. I own it.
7. I love the body I am creating.

8. I am dedicated.
9. Food is Fuel.
10. Weight Loss is certain.

Programming your subconscious to believe in the above statements won't happen by you simply reading these chapters you need to repeat and work on each of these statements daily and as and when scenarios occur to throw you off track use them to help overcome your barriers.

For example, the next time you miss a gym session because you had to work late you need to reaffirm that you have the time to invest in yourself and therefore reschedule your session. If you look in the mirror and are struggling to see improvement you need to affirm that you are in love with the body you are creating. When you are struggling to get motivated and stay focused you need to re-affirm your dedication. The work that you need to put into to ensure weight loss is certain will be a daily task. Affirmations generally can begin to change your subconscious beliefs in as little as three weeks but as a weight loss specialist I generally start to see a shift in mindset around eight to twelve weeks. This is because many fixed beliefs around body image and weight loss were formed at a much younger age and have been affirmed over many years.

Celebrating each win as discussed throughout this book also helps your subconscious mind remain focused on success and achievements. However small or large the win in it all helps towards reaching your end goal and by acknowledging it helps program your mind into bringing your visualisation into reality.

The key to achieving the body you love lies in the belief that you are always improving and not striving for perfection. No week will ever be the perfect week in terms of diet, fitness, mindset, and wellbeing but as long as you're progressing towards the end goal, weight loss is certain. This is where the scales become obsolete because you can be certain that as long as you are progressing the scales will follow, the inch loss will follow, your clothes will fit, and you can be certain that the woman you see in the mirror will improve week on week.

Positive Psychology is already having profound effects on people's success in business, companies pay thousand for training course to see the effects it has their employees and their turnover. Applying the PERMA foundations to your weight loss journey will have the same successful effects. The mantra 'Weight Loss is certain' can be applied to the PERMA theory as summarised below including all the elements we've covered throughout this book. Use these as a reminder to include all the below in your weight loss journey.

P – POSITIVE EMOTION

Your visualisation of the body and lifestyle you are creating builds the positive emotions needed to ensure weight loss is certain.

Positive Affirmations to help remove your limiting beliefs and create new ones.

Focus on self-love and appreciating each and every part of your body

E – ENGAGEMENT

Choosing the physical activities you enjoy and see progression in:

Focusing on personal growth and learning.

Creating a plan that allows you to reach your goals.

R – RELATIONSHIPS

Surrounding yourself with five people who have a positive influence on your journey.

Finding people who inspire you and encourage your progress.

Meeting new people and be willing to learn from them.

M – MEANING

Setting goals that are connected to your lifestyle and wellbeing.

Working towards longer term goals which benefit others i.e. charity walks, runs etc.

Understanding your motivations and connecting to the end goal through visualisations.

A – ACCOMPLISHMENT

Weekly non-critical evaluations to help improve step-by-step.

Celebrating each and every single win and acknowledging progression.

Rewarding yourself through self-care.

I really hope this book has opened your mind up to possibility and you now see the true potential that lies within you to create the body you love with ease.

If you would like to continue to work with me and go deeper into working on your mindset, I'd love to invite you to join me in my studio or attend one of my online workshops or programmes.

I offer body transformations in my studio in Pendle, Lancashire and provide a 1:1 online accountability programme. You can also join us in my MindFIT Academy over on Facebook where we work as group to support each other to achieve our goals. I can't wait to meet you and look forward to getting to know you. I'd love to hear your story and how this book has helped you on your journey.

Weight Loss is certain, queen.

Printed in Great Britain
by Amazon

25961124R00076